COME HOME, INDIO

JIM TERRY

COME HOME, INDIO

A MEMOIR

Street Noise Books
Brooklyn, New York

Library of Congress CIP data available.

ISBN 978-1-951-491-04-8

Edited by Whit Taylor
Book design by Liz Frances

Printed in South Korea

9 8 7 6 5 4 3 2 1

First Edition

For those who are still here.

PART 1

IT WASN'T A *LIE* BUT IT WASN'T THE EXACT TRUTH. IT WAS MY TRUTH, BUT IT WASN'T EVERYTHING.

WHAT'S SO FUNNY?

IT'S PRONOUNCED *IN-DEE-AN*, SON.

WE WERE *STAYING* IN THE HEIGHTS...

THAT'S WHAT I *SAID*...

...BUT IT WAS NEVER WHERE WE *LIVED*.

WELL... PEOPLE LAUGH AT ALL KINDS OF SILLY THINGS.

NOW COME ON... WE'RE ALMOST TO *KUNIKA'S*.

AND THERE IT WAS... THE QUESTION THAT WOULD REMAIN WITH ME FOR YEARS. WERE THEY LAUGHING BECAUSE WHAT I SAID WAS *FUNNY?* OR WERE THEY LAUGHING BECAUSE I THOUGHT I *BELONGED* THERE?

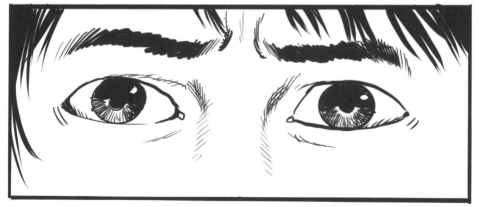

I WASN'T BORN IN WISCONSIN.

I WAS BORN IN *CALIFORNIA*.

5

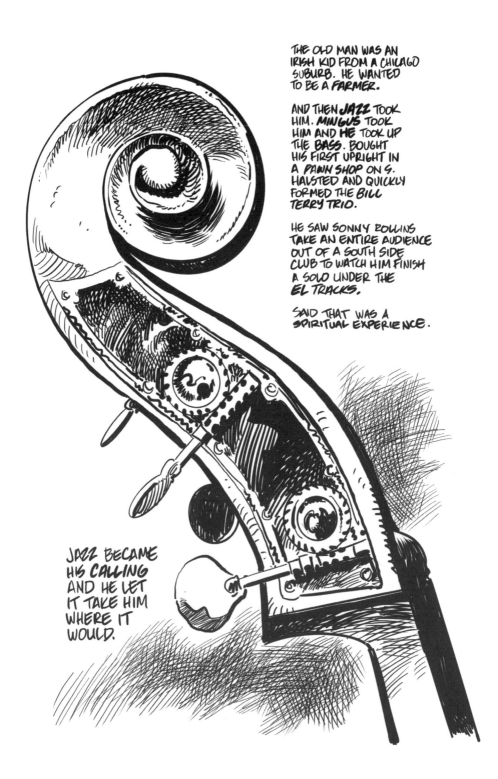

THE OLD MAN WAS AN IRISH KID FROM A CHICAGO SUBURB. HE WANTED TO BE A *FARMER*.

AND THEN *JAZZ* TOOK HIM. *MINGUS* TOOK HIM AND *HE* TOOK UP THE BASS. BOUGHT HIS FIRST UPRIGHT IN A *PAWN* SHOP ON S. HALSTED AND QUICKLY FORMED THE *BILL TERRY TRIO*.

HE SAW SONNY ROLLINS TAKE AN ENTIRE AUDIENCE OUT OF A SOUTH SIDE CLUB TO WATCH HIM FINISH A SOLO UNDER THE EL TRACKS.

SAID THAT WAS A SPIRITUAL EXPERIENCE.

JAZZ BECAME HIS *CALLING* AND HE LET IT TAKE HIM WHERE IT WOULD.

IT TOOK HIM TO NEW YORK, FLORIDA, ARIZONA ...ZIG ZAGGING UNTIL HE HIT *CALIFORNIA*. HIS *SERIOUS LOOK* WAS *PERFECTED* BY THEN AND HE WAS READY TO PLAY SOME MUSIC.

POP WAS THE ONLY SURVIVOR OF *FOUR SONS*. ONE DIED OF PNEUMONIA, ONE WAS HIT BY A *TRAIN*, AND *TOMMY*-THE YOUNGEST AND HIS *BEST FRIEND*- WAS KILLED BY A HIT-AND-RUN DRIVER.

HE GOT TO **L.A.** AND COULDN'T HAVE *CARED LESS* ABOUT *ROCK AND ROLL* OR THE *HIPPIE SCENE*... HE WAS ALL ABOUT *JAZZ* AND THE *NEW* LATIN MUSIC THAT WAS EXPLODING OUT OF *PUERTO RICO* AND *NEW YORK CITY*... **SALSA.**

7

HE WAS A MAN WHO KNEW WHAT HE WAS PUT ON EARTH FOR AND **WORKED** FOR IT.

HE MET MY MOM ON A BRIDGE

SHE ASKED HIM FOR A CIGARETTE

HE ASKED HER ON A DATE

SOON SHE WAS PREGNANT WITH ME AND HIS PATH DISSOLVED

THAT'S HOW *SHE* TOLD IT, ANWAY, THO SHE WAS NEVER ONE TO SHY AWAY FROM A BIT OF *DRAMATIC EMBELLISHMENT.*

A DATE? SURE, MAN.

SHE WAS FROM A DIFFERENT *WORLD* THAN HE WAS. THE FIRST BORN OF EIGHT, SHE COULD RECALL LIVING IN A *CHPÓROKÉ* - A MUD-AND-WOOD SHELTER.

HER CHILDHOOD WASN'T THE EASIEST— KUNIKA WAS AN ACTIVIST AND MOM WAS OFTEN LEFT TO TEND THE HOUSE AND KIDS.

WE'RE HUNGRY...

MOM SAID TO MAKE DINNER.

OKAY ALREADY!

SHE LOVED READING AND MUSIC AND HAD A BEAUTIFUL SINGING VOICE. YEARS LATER SHE SANG THE *NATIONAL ANTHEM* AT A WHITE SOX GAME.

CATHOLIC SCHOOL GIRLS' CHOIR

IN COLLEGE SHE MET A GUY WHO PROMISED HER IT WAS *IMPOSSIBLE* TO GET PREGNANT THE FIRST TIME... HE MUST HAVE *LIED,* BECAUSE NINE MONTHS LATER *TONY* WAS BORN. SHE NEVER SAID MUCH ABOUT HIS DAD.

HE JUST WASN'T IN THE PICTURE.

I CAN'T SAY WHAT MADE HER LEAVE THE DELLS OR WHERE HER TRAVELS TOOK HER...BUT SHE ENDED UP IN L.A.

SHE LEFT HIM WITH HER MOTHER IN WISCONSIN ...A DECISION THAT WOULD FOREVER HAUNT HER.

SOON I WAS ON THE WAY. GRANDMA AND GRANDPA TERRY MADE IT CLEAR— THE ONLY *CHILD* OF THEIR ONLY *SURVIVING* CHILD WAS NOT GOING TO BE BORN A *BASTARD*. THEY WERE PERSUASIVE.

MOM GOT "NEGATIVE VIBES" FROM THEM BUT WASN'T SURE IF IT WAS BECAUSE SHE WAS POOR OR SHE WAS *NATIVE* OR BOTH.

LATER SHE'D PULL ME OUT OF THE *CUB SCOUTS* AND TELL ME IT WAS BECAUSE THEY WERE RACIST AGAINST INDIANS SO FUCK THEM.

I CAN'T SPEAK TO EITHER OF THOSE BUT THE VIBES VANISHED WHEN SHE PLACED A GRANDSON IN THEIR ARMS.

YOU LOSE *THREE* OUT OF *FOUR SONS*... *NOBODY* IS GOING TO BE GOOD ENOUGH. STILL... MOM WAS FROM A COMPLETELY DIFFERENT WORLD.

MY MEMORIES OF CALIFORNIA ARE MUDDY AND FADED, LIKE OLD POLAROIDS.

MADE *TANGIBLE* ONLY THROUGH THE EMBELLISHMENT OF OTHERS.

HEY, THE KID'S GOING UP AGAIN!

ONE MEMORY POP LOVED TO TALK ABOUT WAS THE EVEL KNIEVEL HILL.

SOME BMX COURSE THE LOCAL KIDS DID TRICKS ON. I'D TAKE MY *BIG WHEEL* DOWN IT.

I'D WIPE OUT EVERY TIME AND THE OTHER KIDS WOULD GO SILENT.

C'MON, MI HIJO!

I'D DRAMATICALLY RISE AND THOSE KIDS WOULD CHEER AS I TACKLED IT AGAIN.

YEAH! ALRIGHT KID! WHOO HOO!

IT'S HOW HE ALWAYS TOLD IT.

JIMMY!

MOM JUST SAW IT AS DUMB, RECKLESS ENDANGERMENT.

ARE YOU *CRAZY* LETTING HIM DO THAT, BILL?!?

GAH!

THERE WERE RIFTS FROM THE GET-GO. POP HUNG OUT WITH HIS BUDDIES AND WAS GONE MUCH OF THE TIME. AN UNDERWHELMING DEGREE OF MUTUAL TRUST AND A LOT OF TIME APART WAS THE NORM.

MOST OF MOM'S FRIENDS WERE GAY MEN FOR MANY REASONS. POP DIDN'T CARE FOR THEIR COMPANY, AND HE DID NOT GET JEALOUS OF THEM.

THEY BOTH, HOWEVER, TALKED FONDLY OF THE DESERT AND THE SURROUNDING MOUNTAINS.

IN THE PHOTOS IT'S WHERE THEY SEEMED THE HAPPIEST.

MY **KUNIKA** (GRANDMOTHER) TOLD ME THAT WHILE IN THE WOMB MY WRISTS GOT WRAPPED IN THE UMBILICAL CORD...

...WHICH IS WHY, SHE SAID, I GREW TO BE AN **ARTIST**.

AND, I'D TELL MYSELF LATER, WHY I'D BEEN CURSED WITH SUCH SKINNY, UNMANLY WRISTS.

A YEAR AND A HALF **LATER** MY **SISTER** WAS BORN. POP WAS MAKING A **NAME** FOR HIMSELF IN THE **MUSIC SCENE**... BUT HE WAS NOW IN HIS **THIRTIES** WITH **THREE MOUTHS TO FEED**.

NOT LONG AFTER, WE LEFT **PACOIMA** FOR **CHICAGO**, TO BE CLOSE TO HIS **PARENTS**.

BEFORE WE **LEFT**, MY OLD MAN PUT ME ON HIS **SHOULDERS** TO SAY GOODBYE TO THE **BATMAN PALM TREE**.
I DON'T KNOW HOW IT GOT THAT NAME, BUT IT HAD **SOME** KIND OF SIGNIFICANCE – IT SEEMED SPECIAL TO ME.

WE WENT TO THE PARK TO SEE IT.

LOOK AT IT, JIMMY. REMEMBER IT.

YOU MIGHT NEVER SEE IT AGAIN.

I REMEMBER IT SWAYING, MAYBE A THOUSAND MILES UP AND **SILENT**.

WE STOOD LIKE THAT FOR A WHILE, UNTIL I FELT A TIGHT ACHE THAT I WOULD LATER IDENTIFY AS **MELANCHOLY**.

WE'D BE FRIENDS FOR **LIFE**, THAT FEELING AND I.

POP SAID GOODBYE TO HIS FRIENDS AND HIS CAREER TRAJECTORY. HE WAS LEAVING IT ALL.

MOM SAID GOODBYE TO THE FRIENDS SHE'D MADE. SHE WAS BEING PULLED BACK TOWARD THE WOODS.

MOM AND ELENA TOOK A PLANE BACK TO CHICAGO...

...POP PACKED THE TRUCK AND WE STARTED OUR CROSS-COUNTRY ROAD TRIP.

I DON'T THINK HE EVER WENT BACK TO CALIFORNIA.

14

POP AND I CROSSED THE COUNTRY TOGETHER IN THE OLD BLUE **TRUCK**, THE ONE WITHOUT *HUBCAPS*.

WE ALWAYS HAD A TRUCK.

AS AN OLDER, SEMI-RETIRED *MAN* HE BOUGHT A *COMPACT CAR* — AND LOOKED ODD IN IT... *UNNATURAL*.

LOOK AT THOSE MOUNTAINS, JIMMY!

I RECALL STANDING ON THE SEAT OF THAT TRUCK, FEELING PERFECTLY SAFE.

I DO **NOT**, HOWEVER, RECALL SHITTING MY PANTS IN OKLAHOMA CITY.

AWE, COME **ON**, MAN!

...BUT APPARENTLY I *DID*.

WE STOPPED AT A **STORE** TO GET SOME NEW PANTS. I GUESS POP DIDN'T **PLAN** FOR... ACCIDENTS.

GENERAL STORE

MAN, JIMMY, COULDN'T YOU HOLD IT? WHY DIDN'T YOU TELL ME YOU HAD TO GO?

BUT THEN HE STARTED NOTICING THE LOOKS HE WAS GETTING FROM THE LARGELY *NATIVE POPULATION*...

GULP...

I...WANT *MOMMY!*

THEY...THEY THINK I STOLE JIMMY! THEY THINK SOME *WHITE GUY* KIDNAPPED AN INDIAN KID!

WE QUICKLY GOT WHAT WAS NEEDED AND WERE THE **HELL OUT** OF THERE... AND THE OKLAHOMA CITY PANTS POOPING INCIDENT PASSED INTO **LEGEND**.   UNFORTUNATELY.

YOU KNOW, KID...

..."YOU COULD'A HELPED YER OLD MAN OUT A LITTLE, BACK THERE.

LOOK AT THOSE MOUNTAINS!

WE MOVED INTO A *RANCH* HOUSE IN THE SOUTHWEST SUBURBS OF *CHICAGO*, A FEW MILES FROM MY DAD'S PARENTS. GRAMMA SOLD *REAL ESTATE*, AND I'M SURE THEY SECURED THE PLACE.

THE BLOCK WAS QUIET, AND BEHIND THE BACK YARD WAS A STRETCH OF UNTOUCHED FIELD, ALMOST PRAIRIE.

OUR NEIGHBOR, MR. ANDERSON, WORKED AT THE HERSHEY CHOCOLATE FACTORY AND WOULD SOMETIMES GIVE US BAGS OF CANDY BARS-WHICH MY DAD WOULD QUICKLY CONFISCATE.

"YOU'LL ROT YOUR TEETH."

HE'D TAKE THEM AND EAT THEM IN THE GARAGE.

YEARS LATER WHEN MR. ANDERSON COULD NO LONGER WALK, POP WOULD THROW ME TEN BUCKS TO MOW HIS LAWN... WHICH I'D IMMEDIATELY SPEND ON COMICS AND CANDY.

POP GOT A JOB WITH AL PIERSON, PLAYING UPRIGHT **BASS** IN HIS **BIG BAND**. HE'D BE GONE FOR SEVERAL WEEKS AT A TIME.

I DON'T THINK I WAS EVER **TOO** SAD WHEN HE'D LEAVE. WE WERE FREE TO DO OTHER THINGS, ALL THE STUFF HE DIDN'T GET *INTO*.

IT WAS **MOM** WHO INTRODUCED ME TO THE **ARTS**. THE THEATER WAS A **HOME** TO ME.

SHE WAS *ALWAYS READING* AND KEPT ME IN COMICS AND BOOKS. MY CHILDHOOD WITH HER WAS THE QUIET SOUND OF PAGES TURNING.

WE WERE BROKE, BUT SOMEHOW SHE ALWAYS FOUND THE **DOUGH** FOR WHAT WOULD *FEED MY* **BRAIN.**

ONCE WE SAT THROUGH **"RAIDERS OF THE LOST ARK"** TWO TIMES IN A ROW. I WAS WORRIED WE WERE DOING SOMETHING WRONG WHEN THE PLACE *EMPTIED BETWEEN SCREENINGS*...

YEARS LATER I REALIZED WE WEREN'T STAYING FOR ME, BUT FOR *HARRISON FORD*. AH WELL.

THE BEST WAS GOING UP TO THE *DELLS*. IT WAS THE LAND OF TREES AND GO-CARTS AND *SWIMMING* AND *RUNNING AROUND* AND THE FEEL OF THE SUN TIGHTENING YOUR SKIN AND GRASS UNDER BARE FEET. AND MOST OF ALL....

IT WAS AN AGONIZING *FOUR HOUR DRIVE* FROM OUR HOUSE TO THE INDIAN HEIGHTS.

I USED TO HAVE A *DREAM* THAT WE HAD DISCOVERED A *MAGIC PATH* THROUGH A CORNFIELD THAT GOT US THERE IN *MINUTES*.

I COULDN'T WAIT TO SEE MY TEGAS (UNCLES), MOMS (AUNTS), ALL MY BROTHERS AND SISTERS... THERE IS NO SUCH THING AS A *COUSIN* IN "INDIAN WAY."

AND *TONY* WAS THERE.

KUNIKA'S HOUSE SEEMED LIKE THE CENTER OF ACTION IN THE HEIGHTS, AND THAT IS WHERE TONY STAYED. ACCORDING TO MY MOM, DAD COULD NEVER GET PAST THE FACT THAT TONY WAS ANOTHER MAN'S SON.

TONY!

BARK BARK

WHICH WAS WHY HE WASN'T WITH US IN ILLINOIS.

HEY LITTLE BROTHER!

MOM, LOOK!

TONY LIFTED ME OFF THE GROUND!

DEB.

J.T. AND ELENA ARE HERE!

TONY HAD LEUKEMIA.

I'M GONNA LIFT ELENA TOO, WATCH!

EVERYONE KNEW HE WOULD SOON BE GONE.

IT WAS ONLY A MATTER OF TIME. UNTIL THEN, WE PLAYED.

ONE DAY WHEN I WAS SIX POP CAME OUT OF THE HOUSE AND THREW ME IN THE TRUCK. WE HEADED NORTH IN SILENCE - MOM AND ELENA WERE ALREADY UP THERE - I'M NOT SURE WE EVEN *PACKED* A TOOTHBRUSH.

I WAS TERRIFIED.

ALONG THE WAY HE TREATED ME TO A&W, WHICH SCARED ME EVEN MORE.

HE NEVER DID THAT BEFORE, HE HATED FAST FOOD.

IT WAS TONY, HE WAS GONE.

NINE YEARS OLD. WHEN HE LEFT I THINK IT *BROKE* SOMETHING IN MY MOM THAT NEVER TRULY HEALED.

MY SECRET, SHAMEFUL FEAR WAS THAT I WOULD ALSO DIE ONCE I TURNED NINE.

I WAS RELIEVED WHEN I TURNED TEN AND DEEPLY ASHAMED THAT I'D EVER *HAD* THE FEAR.

BUT I THINK MY BIG BROTHER WOULD HAVE UNDERSTOOD AND FORGIVEN ME.

LIKE A SUDDEN STORM THERE WAS MISERY IN THE AIR AND POWERFUL, COMPLICATED EMOTIONS I DIDN'T UNDERSTAND. GRIEF, PAIN, AND *LOSS* WERE *NEW* AND CONFLICT WAS BECOMING *FAMILIAR* — SHROUDED IN A *FUME OF BOOZE* AND *ANGER*. TENSION AND UNCERTAINTY BECAME NORMAL.

A *KNOT* COILED IN MY GUT AND DIDN'T GO AWAY.

ELENA WAS THE ONLY *CONSTANT* AND WE *LEANED* ON EACH OTHER WITHOUT *KNOWING* IT. LAUGHTER THROUGH THE TEARS.

EVENTUALLY IT WAS *BACK* TO *ILLINOIS* WITH A MALIGNANT *CLOUD* HANGING OVER THE FAMILY.

GUILT, BLAME, SHAME, AND ANGER.

WE WERE HELPLESS AGAINST THE WEIGHT OF HER SADNESS, UNABLE TO COMPETE WITH WHATEVER SHE SEARCHED FOR IN THE MIDDLE DISTANCE, AND IT WAS UNSETTLING.

DAD SPENT A LOT OF TIME IN THE *GARAGE* WHEN HE WAS HOME, AND WAS ALWAYS *DIFFERENT* WHEN HE CAME OUT.

I ALWAYS FELT THERE *HAD* TO BE SOMETHING I COULD DO.

I NEVER REALLY LEARNED THAT THERE WASN'T.

PLAYFUL OR WITHDRAWN.

SILLY OR ANGRY.

IT WAS A *CRAP SHOOT* AND I SOON LEARNED TO HOLD MY *BREATH* UNTIL I COULD READ THE SITUATION.

WHEN THE SPIRITS WERE *GOOD* HE'D *LAUGH* AND PLAY HIS *CONGAS* AND ELENA AND I WOULD TRY AND *DANCE* WHILE HE *CRACKED UP* AND ENCOURAGED US.

YEAH MAN, YEAH!

HA HA, FAR OUT, KIDS!

BOOM BUM BUM BOOM

23

THERE WAS PLENTY TO FEAR, GROWING UP. MOSTLY FEARS LEARNED FROM *MOVIES*.

SCORPIONS...
QUICKSAND...
TORNADOES...
POISON...
THE DEVIL...
CAR CRASHES...

EARTHQUAKES
BODY SNATCHERS
LEATHERFACE
VENUS FLYTRAP
SO MUCH TO BE
TERRIFIED OF!

THERE WERE ALSO *OTHER* FEARS. THINGS BEYOND MY UNDERSTANDING... *NATIVE THINGS*.

WHEN YOU *HIDE* AT NIGHT SPIRITS HIDE *WITH* YOU. SO *STOP* TRYING TO SCARE YOUR SISTER.

!

STOP LOOKING IN PEOPLES' WINDOWS - YOU WANT BAD THINGS TO START HANGING AROUND YOU?

!
NO...

RAWR! MOM *LOOK* I'M BIGFOOT!

BIGFOOT IS *REAL*, HONEY.

...HE IS?

THE SHINING

MOM LISTEN, I CAN WHISTLE THE "STAR WARS" SONG.

DON'T EVER WHISTLE AFTER DARK! SPIRITS!

(GULP)
OKAY,
OKAY!

AND THERE WAS THE FEAR TO END ALL OTHERS. AN OWL, A SPIRIT KNOWN AS THE *HOMPOOK*.

YOU WANNA CRY? OKAY FINE THEN, THE HOMPOOK WILL HEAR YOU AND THINK YOU'RE CALLING HIM, YOU WANT HIM TO COME FOR YOU?

(SNIFF)
N-NOO...

THE HOMPOOK FROZE ME WITH FEAR.

TINGLING WITH TERROR IN BED, SURE IT WAS WATCHING ME JUST OUTSIDE THE *WINDOW*... WAITING PATIENT AND SILENT FOR THE SOUND OF MY CRYING SO IT COULD TAKE ME.

AND YET NOT NEARLY AS REAL AS THE SOUND OF THOSE MEANT TO *PROTECT* YOU LOSING CONTROL.

YELLING. FIGHTING. *DRUNK*. ALL SENSE OF SAFETY AND ORDER *SHREDDED* IN ANGRY BABBLE.

SOMETIMES THERE WOULD BE A STRANGE SOUND AND THEN IT'D BE SILENT AS A TOMB.

I'D PULL THE COVERS OVER MY HEAD AND WAIT FOR THE MORNING.

AND THE HOMPOOK RELEGED TO A SILLY TALL TALE.

MEMORIES OF THEM *TOGETHER* ARE FEW. MOSTLY I CAN PICTURE THE *LIVING ROOM.*

IMAGINE A *BOOK* IN WHICH THE CHARACTERS GET *DRUNK* BUT ARE *NEVER SEEN* DRINKING.

CHAPTER BY CHAPTER THEY CHANGE. THEY GET *LOUDER* OR *WITHDRAWN...* *AFFECTIONATE* OR *AGGRESSIVE* - BUT WITH NO EXPLANATION OR *REASON.*

IT IS *BAFFLING* AND *TERRIFYING.*

WHAT'RE YA DRAWIN' NOW, JIMMY?

JUST... THE NUMBER FIVE...

YOU ALWAYS LET HIM JUST WASTE PAPER LIKE THAT, DEBBIE?! THINK MONEY JUST GROWS ON *TREES!?!?* HUH?

BILL, IT'S JUST PAPER.

OH YEAH? MAKES ME WONDER WHAT ELSE GOES ON WHEN I'M NOT AROUND!

THERE WAS NO WAY TO PREDICT WHEN THINGS WOULD GET BAD OR WHY OR *HOW* BAD. I DIDN'T UNDERSTAND HOW THEY COULD TURN INTO *COMPLETELY DIFFERENT PEOPLE* ONCE THE *NIGHT* FELL AND THE STINK OF ALCOHOL BECAME THEIR SMELL, SOUR AND SICK.

LIKE A SKIN COMING OFF OR A SHADOW PASSING OVER A FACE, THEY WERE SUDDENLY *STRANGERS* TO THEIR CHILDREN.

ONE NIGHT THINGS GOT VERY BAD. ELENA AND I ESCAPED OUT THE BATHROOM WINDOW AND RAN THROUGH THE SNOW TO A *SYMPATHETIC NEIGHBOR'S* HOUSE.

BEFORE WE KNEW IT LIFE SPLIT IN *TWO*. A VOID ENTERED POP'S HOUSE. THE BOOKS WERE GONE AND SO WAS THE TENDERNESS - IF I FELL I NO LONGER CRIED FOR ATTENTION - I JUST PRETENDED IT DIDN'T *HURT*.

MOM WAS LIVING WITH A MAN NAMED *DON* WHO WAS YOUNG, TALL, AND SMART. THEY MET DRIVING *SCHOOL* BUSES. THEY SPENT THEIR NIGHTS *DRINKING*.

EVERYTHING I TOLD THE COUNCELOR WAS USED LIKE A *WEAPON* IN COURT. MOM LOST THE CUSTODY BATTLE AND THAT WAS USED AS A WEAPON TOO.

SORRY, MOM...

IT'S NOT YOUR FAULT, SON.

JESUS, JIM... "SHE DOES LAUNDRY GOOD?!"

THE ACTUAL REASON SHE LOST WAS MY DAD'S PARENTS, GRANDMA AND *GRANDPA*, STEPPED IN ONCE MORE AND COULD AFFORD A *LAWYER*.

IT'S NOT MY FAULT. IT'S *NOT* MY FAULT.

IT'S NOT MY FAULT. IT'S *NOT* MY FAULT!

IT'S NOT MY FAULT, DON. OKAY?

STILL, GUILT RAN *DEEP.* THEY NOW *KNEW* I HATED WHERE THEY LIVED. I HAD BETRAYED THEM SOMEHOW... I BEGAN FIGHTING THE KIDS IN THE *APARTMENT* COMPLEX.

FIGHTS IN SCHOOL WEREN'T UNUSUAL, KIDS ARE PRETTY AWFUL AND I WAS VERY SENSITIVE... BUT I WAS MOSTLY *AFRAID* OF FIGHTING.

YER INDIAN? FEATHERS OR DOTS? HEY-YA-HEY-YA

HA HA HA HA HA HA

WOO WOO!

WHEN I DID I WAS A *MANIAC.* I NEVER "WON" IN ANY WAY.

WHAT'RE YA EATIN', BISON BURG—

SHUT UUP!

I'D JUST SEE RED.

MY GRADES WERE IN THE GUTTER. I WAS FAILING READING, WHICH DON AND MY MOM FOUND UNFORGIVABLE. THEY SAT ME DOWN.

DON'T LIKE READING? OKAY THEN... YOU'RE GROUNDED. FOR THE SUMMER.

I FEEL SICK...

I WAS GIVEN THREE BOOKS TO READ (WITHOUT PICTURES) AND WAS GROUNDED FROM ANYTHING ELSE UNTIL DON THOROUGHLY QUIZZED ME ON THEM.

NO FRIENDS. ATARI. POOL. MOVIES. CARTOONS. COMICS. G.I. JOES. STAR WARS. MATCHBOX. BASEBALL. BIKES. LIFE.

HATING EVERY WORD, I SLOGGED THROUGH "LORD OF THE FLIES", UNDERSTANDING LITTLE.

WHAT'S A CONCH?

STUPID STUPID BOOK!

I RAGED, FUMBLING THROUGH THE STRANGE "ONE FLEW OVER THE CUCKOO'S NEST."

IT'S NOT FAIR!

I JUST DON'T GET IT!!

FINALLY, "FLOWERS FOR ALGERNON." IT BEGAN AS THOUGH WRITTEN BY A CHILD.

WELL HERE GOES. ONE MORE STUPID BOOK LEFT.

HMM... WEIRD. WONDER WHY THE WRITING IS LIKE THIS?

AS THE NARRATOR GREW SMARTER AND THE WRITING CHANGED SOMETHING IN MY BRAIN UNLOCKED. I DEVOURED THE BOOK.

MY STOMACH IS IN A KNOT... I DON'T WANT THIS TO END SAD! I...DON'T WANT IT TO END.

THEY REALLY SHOULD TEACH ROGER WATERS IN SCHOOL. DO YOU LIKE IT?

IT'S KIND OF SCARY.

OKAY, TIME TO DISCOVER NEIL YOUNG, THEN.

PINK FLOYD THE WALL

BEING A *JAZZ MAN*, DAD DIDN'T *LIKE* THIS OUTSIDE INFLUENCE. HE DIDN'T *HIDE* IT.

YOU KNEW WE PLANNED HIS BIRTHDAY PARTY AT FOUR, BILL. IT'S ALMOST FIVE, IT'S PRETTY MUCH OVER.

YEAH, WELL, SORRY HE'S A LITTLE LATE.

OH WELL. IT'S HIS PARTY YOU RUINED.

GET ON IN, SON.

MOST OF THE TIME I FELT JUST BENEATH DON'S NOTICE OR IN HIS GOOD GRACES, BUT IT DIDN'T TAKE MUCH FOR HIS INTELLECT TO TURN MEAN.

FINE, JIM. DEFEND YOUR DAD. THE MAN WHO COULDN'T EVEN ACCEPT TONY AND FORCED YOUR MOM TO—

DONALD! PLEASE!

SHUT... UP...

LIKE MOST ADULTS, HE WAS A BAFFLING PUZZLE TO ME, WITH HIDDEN PIECES. WARM OR FRIGHTENING WITH NO WARNING OR CLUE.

YEAH, RIGHT THERE ABOVE THE KNEECAP. NEXT TIME SOMEONE CALLS YOU AN *INJUN*, JUST HOOK YOUR HEEL IN AND KICK DOWN. RIGHT THERE.

THIS FROM THE ARMY?

UH-HUH.

DONALD! DON'T TEACH HIM TO CRIPPLE PEOPLE!

MUSTACHE RIDES FREE

I WOULD LIE IN BED, PICTURING THE WORLD DISINTEGRATING. I COULDN'T UNDERSTAND HOW PEOPLE — *JUST PEOPLE!* — COULD HOLD THAT OVER US ALL.

AS I WAS ABOUT TO GIVE INTO *CRUSHING DESPAIR* AND *HOPELESSNESS* ~ THEY ASKED A "DUDE."

WOW, MAN, NEVER REALLY THOUGHT ABOUT IT, BUT...

...WELL I GUESS I'D JUST GRAB A CHAIR, SIT ON THE ROOF AND WATCH IT ALL, YA KNOW?

I MEAN IT'S NOT SOMETHING YOU'LL EVER SEE *TWICE* HA HA HA HA!

MY HERO. SOMEONE WHO HAD IT ALL *FIGURED OUT.* I CLUNG TO HIS RIDICULOUS CONFIDENCE, HIS COMPLETE LACK OF FEAR UNTIL MY *OWN* TERROR BEGAN TO SUBSIDE. WHAT *FREEDOM!*

WELL, UH, THERE YOU HAVE IT FOLKS...WE BRING YOU AGAIN ~.

BREA...ATH

THANK YOU FOR THAT, DUDE. WHOEVER, WHEREVER YOU MIGHT BE.

THANK YOU FOR YOUR *RADICAL ACCEPTANCE* AND HELPING ME TO GET A *GOOD NIGHT'S SLEEP.*

FUCK IT.

ZZZZ

DON'S TOENAILS WERE CURVED, LIKE SNAIL SHELLS. WHILE READING HE WOULD *PICK* AT THEM, ABSENTLY.

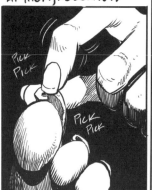

PICK PICK

PICK PICK

ELENA AND I HAD A *MORBID FASCINATION* WITH THEM.

YESSS?

HUH? NOTHIN'.

I TERRORIZED HER ABOUT THOSE THINGS.

DON'S TOENAILS...COMIN' TO *GETCHA!* HA HAA!

STOP!

SUDDENLY THE SOUND OF MOM AND DON'S LATE NIGHT *PARTYING* WOULD STOP AND WE'D FREEZE AS HE CHECKED ON US.

MELLOW...

SNORE...

ONCE THE DOOR CLOSED I'D GO RIGHT BACK TO IT WITH *FRESH MATERIAL*...

MELLOW YELLOW COMIN' TO *GETCHA!*

STOP IT!

...

UH...

MELLOW.

SNORE...

USUALLY THEY DRANK AT THE DINNER TABLE BUT SOMETIMES THEY'D JUST DISAPPEAR. ON *WEEKENDS* THEY'D DRINK WITH OUR NEIGHBOR *RUSS* AND HIS WIFE, WHO ELENA AND I DID NOT LIKE. MOM LATER TOLD ME RUSS WAS A *SWINGER.* I QUICKLY STOPPED HER FROM TELLING ME *ANY* MORE.

DID YOU SEE THE PATCH ON RUSS'S JEANS?

!

EWN...

DON'T STOP

...GROSS. WHY DO THEY HANG OUT WITH SUCH A WEIRDO? JEEZ!

I DON'T KNOW.

WHEN WE MOVED TO A *NEW* APARTMENT THEY WOULDN'T HIDE IT, THEY'D JUST *LEAVE.*

...JIM?

YEAH?

I THINK THEY'RE *GONE* AGAIN.

ELENA AND I WOULD GO TO THE LIVING ROOM AND SIT IN THE *DARK,* WATCHING THE CARS PULL INTO THE PARKING LOT BELOW.

IS *THAT* THEM?

NO...

JIM... WHAT IF THEY'RE *DEAD?*

I DON'T KNOW.

WHEN THEY *DID* PULL IN - SOMETIMES LAUGHING, SOMETIMES YELLING - I WAS FLOODED WITH *RELIEF...* AND *ANGER.*

THERE THEY ARE.

PHEW!

WE'D RUN BACK TO BED AND SOON ONE OF THEM WOULD *CHECK* ON US, REEKING OF CIGARETTES AND *BOOZE.*

KEEP SLEEPING, MY BABIESH... I LOVE YOU...

YEAH, RIGHT!

BETTER WITH AGE

OTHER TIMES IT GOT WORSE.

YEARS LATER I WAS WATCHING "ONCE WERE WARRIORS" WITH A GIRLFRIEND, ABOUT MAORIS IN *NEW ZEALAND.*

DURING A SCENE OF DOMESTIC VIOLENCE THEY CUT TO THE CHILDREN, HUDDLED TOGETHER IN *FEAR*, HELPLESS.

BEFORE I KNEW WHAT WAS HAPPENING I WAS SOBBING UNCONTROLLABLY.

I COULD NOT EXPLAIN IT TO HER AND WAS SO OVERCOME WITH SUDDEN *SHAME* THAT I WOULDN'T HAVE ANYWAY.

I HATE THE SONG "DESPERADO" BY THE EAGLES.

MOM?

YES, IT'S A GARBAGE TUNE THAT ROMANTICIZES BULLSHIT... BUT THAT'S NOT WHY I HATE IT.

WHY DON'T YOU COME TO... (SOB) YOUR SENSES...

IT WAS THAT RAW DRUNKEN CONNECTION SHE HAD TO IT.

YOU BETTER LET SOMEBODY LOVE YOU...

IT FILLED ME WITH SHAME AND ANGER AND DISGUST. HOW DARE SHE LET ME SEE HER SO WEAK? I WAS SICK OF IT AND POWERLESS. A FORCED OBSERVER.

IN THE LIGHT OF DAY EVERYTHING FELT JUST FINE.
THE HOT SUN BURNED AWAY RESIDUAL ANGER
AND *SHAME* LIKE MORNING *FOG*, AND I BECAME
ACCUSTOMED TO THE FLICKERING SENSE OF
TENSION AND *UNEASE* IN MY STOMACH.

THERE WAS ALSO A WHISPER IN MY MIND, A
GROWING IDEA THAT SOMEWHERE I'D DONE
SOMETHING *WRONG* AND IT'D CHANGED HOW
MOM *FELT* ABOUT ME.

WHY ELSE WOULD SHE ALWAYS SEEM SO UNHAPPY?

IT *HAD* TO BE SOMETHING I'D DONE.

DAD ALWAYS SEEMED *ANGRY* WHEN HE PICKED US UP, MOSTLY ABOUT THE TWENTY-MINUTE *DRIVE* BUT HE WAS JUST *ANGRY*.

MAN, YOU GUYS STINK LIKE SMOKE!

IT'S NOT OUR FAULT! THEY SMOKE A LOT!

OK, OK.

HOWEVER LIFE COULDN'T HAVE BEEN *MORE DIFFERENT* ONCE WE WERE AT POP'S - THE *TV* WAS *NEVER* ON UNLESS THE *CUBS* WERE PLAYING THAT DAY.

ALL RIGHT, GO PLAY OUTSIDE! I'LL MAKE YOU SOME LUNCH.

YEAH!

I COULD ALWAYS HEAR HIM *WHISTLING* IN THE KITCHEN THROUGH THE OPEN WINDOW AS HE *COOKED*. HE DESPISED FAST FOOD AND MADE *ALL* OUR MEALS.

♫♪

STOP IT!

HA HA HA!

FOOD ALWAYS TASTED BETTER AFTER PLAYING OUTSIDE IN THE *SUN* ALL DAY.

♪

WHILE WE ATE HE'D WHISTLE AND CLEAN.

HE'D "PUTTER AROUND" IN HIS GARDEN WHILE WE PLAYED UNTIL IT GOT *DARK*.

DAMN WEEDS.

THEY WERE GOOD, HEALTHY DAYS AND AT NIGHT I WOULD READ WITH THE WINDOWS OPEN AND THE NIGHT BREEZE WAFTING IN UNTIL SLEEP CAME.

SNOOORE

ONE SUMMER DAY ELENA AND I WERE DIGGING A HOLE IN THE BACKYARD FOR NO GOOD REASON WHEN WE MADE A *MAGICAL DISCOVERY.*

JIM, LOOK... IT'S **TURQUOISE!!!**

WHOA, REALLY?

UH-HUH!

WE CAN GIVE IT TO *KUNIKA* AND SHE'LL MAKE IT INTO JEWELRY!

WE'LL BE RICH! KEEP DIGGING!

DAD!!

WHAT?! C'MON I GOT A *GIG* TONIGHT! WHATTAYA WANT?

DAD WE DISCOVERED TURQUOISE IN THE BACK YARD AND WE'RE GONNA *MINE* IT ALL AND GIVE IT TO KUNIKA SO SHE CAN MAKE STUFF TO SELL WITH IT!

YEAH, OKAY.

OKAY THANKS DAD LOVE YOU BYE!

YEARS LATER I ASKED HIM ABOUT THAT AND HE **LAUGHED.** "THE GOLDFISH DIED AND I DIDN'T HAVE THE HEART TO TELL YOU KIDS, SO I BURIED THE WHOLE THING, ROCKS AND ALL. IT KEPT YOU BUSY, SO I JUST LET YOU HAVE FUN FOR A BIT."

WHOA, LOOK AT THIS ONE!

YEAH, SHE CAN MAKE A NECKLACE WITH THAT ONE PROLLY.

42

POP DID HIS BEST TO MAKE SURE WE DIDN'T GROW UP KNOWING NOTHING BUT THE SUBURBS SO WE SPENT A LOT OF TIME IN THE *CITY*.

HE HAD PLENTY OF *LADY FRIENDS* THAT WE'D GO VISIT. I LOVED THE FOOD THEY'D COOK AND THEY USUALLY HAD KIDS OUR AGE TO PLAY WITH.

OKAY, INDIO. WHAT STOP WE TRANSFER AT? C'MON, KID.

UH... CLARK?

NO, MAN. WASHINGTON. YOU GOTTA PAY ATTENTION!

RUMBLE

BEEP

HONK HONK

SCREECH

WHO WANTS MORE RICE AND BEANS? YIMMY?

YES, PLEASE!

POR FAVOR. MAN, THIS KID JUST DON'T WANT TO LEARN.

SORRY, OKAY?! ¡POR FAVOR! OKAY?!

THE CITY WAS *DANGEROUS* AND HE WANTED US TO UNDERSTAND THAT. WE'D BEEN ROBBED IN THE STREET, THE BUS WE WERE RIDING GOT CAUGHT IN THE MIDDLE OF A SHOOT-OUT... I SAW A KID GET KILLED BY A CAR COMING OUT OF AN ALLEY.

"YOU GOTTA PAY ATTENTION, JIMMY. THE STREETS WILL *CHEW* YOU UP."

I WAS OFTEN VERY SCARED BUT KNEW WITHIN THAT HE WOULDN'T LET ANYTHING HAPPEN TO US. HE KNEW THE WORLD WAS TOUGH.

WILLIAM, BE CAREFUL!

HA HA, HE'S FINE.

MY TURN!

AND I KNEW HE HAD US.

HA HA HA HA HA!!

ON NIGHTS HE'D HAD TOO MANY IT WAS FEAR-OF HIS *DRIVING*, OF HIS *CHANGING MOODS*, OF ANYTHING THAT MIGHT STRIKE HIS FANCY.

CHECK IT OUT, AN OPEN HYDRANT!

INDIO, GO OUT THERE, MAN! GO PLAY! YOU LOVE WATER!

HUH?

BUT I DON'T HAVE SWIMMING TRUNKS!

JUST GO IN YER UNDERWEAR, MAN, NOBODY CARES.

C'MON KID, GO HAVE FUN!

HA HA HA!

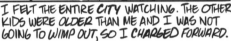

I HATED BEING PUSHED BUT WHEN HE **DRANK** HE WAS RELENTLESS. HE SAW *FREEDOM* AND *FUN*, I SAW HUMILIATION AND SHAME.

GO GET 'EM, MI HIJO.... EVEL KNIEVEL!

I FELT THE ENTIRE *CITY* WATCHING. THE OTHER KIDS WERE *OLDER* THAN ME AND I WAS NOT GOING TO *WIMP OUT*, SO I *CHARGED FORWARD*.

WHOA-SLOW DOWN, KID!

UH OH

THE WATER HIT ME AND FLIPPED ME LIKE A *COIN*. I LANDED IN THE STREET AND RAN BACK TO THE TRUCK BEFORE I COULD HEAR THEM *LAUGH*.

!

YOU GONNA **MOPE** THE WHOLE WAY HOME? CAN'T BE *SUCH* A **CRYBABY** ALL THE TIME, MAN. YOU DID IT. SHOULD BE PROUD.

YOU WENT FLYING!

POP WANTED US TO APPRECIATE *NATURE*, SO WE'D PACK UP THE *TRUCK* AND HEAD TO THE *COUNTRY* TO *FISH* AND *HIKE* AND *BBQ*.

SEE GUYS? COUNTRY FOLK ARE DIFFERENT. FRIENDLIER. YOU WAVE TO EACH OTHER OUT HERE.

JIMMY GET YOUR FACE OUTTA THAT DAMN BOOK AND LOOK AROUND, MAN!

AT WHAT, DAD? IT'S *FARMS* IS ALL! FARMS!

BOY... LOOK AT THAT SUNSET, HUH, KIDS? MOTHER NATURE SURE IS SOMETHING.

WOW!

MY BOOK...

HE WAS DOING HIS *BEST* AND ALWAYS *WOULD*... BUT VISIONS OF THINGS I'D SEEN WOULD FLARE UP AND SOUR IT ALL. HE WAS OFTEN BAFFLED BY THIS.

GETTING *LATE*... LET'S HEAD HOME! MAN, THAT CLEAN 'COUNTRY' AIR MAKES YOU TIRED, HUH?

STOP TRYIN' TO MAKE ME LIKE STUFF.

45

DRINKING DAD WAS ANOTHER STORY. HE KNEW I'D BEEN GETTING IN *FIGHTS* SO HE GOT US *BOXING GLOVES* AND STOOD ME IN THE LIVING ROOM. I COULD SMELL THE BOOZE FUMES.

OKAY SON I'M GONNA TEACH YOU HOW TO *FIGHT*.

DO I HAVE TO?

JAZZ OR *SALSA* USUALLY *DISTRACTED* HIM BUT WHEN IT WAS QUIET LIKE THIS HIS FOCUS WAS *INTENSE*.

WHAT KINDA — *YES!* NOW SHOW ME HOW YOU THROW A *PUNCH*.

...I DON'T WANT TO...

WHY DID THEY DRINK? THEY NEVER SEEMED *HAPPIER* WHEN DRUNK... JUST *SAD* OR *ANGRY*. AND *MEAN*.

DON'T BE A *SISSY*, NO SON OF MINE'S GONNA GET PUSHED AROUND LIKE A LITTLE *FAIRY*... C'MON, *SISSY*.

I'M NOT THAT!

PROVE IT!

I HATED IT. I WOULD *NEVER* BE LIKE THEM.

C'MON, PUNK — SHOW ME WHAT YOU GOT!

WHUD

OKAY THEN!

THERE YOU GO, MAN!

ALL RIGHT ALI! USE YOUR FEET, JUST LIKE *ROCKY*!

AAR!

47

WHAT WAS ALL THIS BUSINESS ABOUT BEING A MAN? HOW DID ONE GO ABOUT *ACHIEVING* IT? DID *FIGHTING* MAKE ME A MAN? IF SO....

...I WASN'T VERY *GOOD* AT BEING A MAN.

DID *SEXUAL EXPERIENCE* MAKE ONE A MAN? LOCKER-ROOM *BRAGS* AND THE VICIOUS WAYS JOCKS TALKED OF THEIR EXPLOITS EMBARRASSED ME. IT DIDN'T FEEL LIKE *GRATITUDE* THAT SOMEONE WOULD HAVE THEM, IT JUST FELT LIKE *CRUELTY*. I LOATHED THE "CONQUERER".

IT MAY HAVE BEEN SIMPLE *JEALOUSY* : THOSE GUYS ALWAYS SEEMED GOOD LOOKING AND *LESS THAN POOR*.

ALL GOOD REASONS, IN MY MIND, TO *DISLIKE* THEM.

YEAH DUDE, WE WERE IN HER BASE- MENT AND I JUST SAID, "YOU SHOULD JUST PUT ...

HA HA YEAH.

SHUT UP!

WAS IT *KILLING*? I ONCE KNOCKED A BIRD OFF ITS BRANCH WITH MY *BB GUN* - IT MADE ME SICK TO MY STOMACH. IT HAD DONE *NO WRONG*.

HUNTING WAS IN MY *CULTURE* AND MY *TEGAS* ASKED ME TO *JOIN* THEM FOR DEER SEASON.

THOUGH I KNEW THE MEAT WOULD BE USED I COULD NEVER BRING MYSELF TO GO.

OH GOD... YOU WERE JUST SITTING THERE CHIRPING. WHY DID I *DO* THIS?

I'M SO SORRY...

WAS IT *COURAGE*, PERHAPS? AS A SMALL BOY I WAS HANDED A RAW *TURTLE HEART* AND TOLD BY MY *TEGAS* IT WOULD MAKE ME *STRONG*.

AT THEIR INSTRUCTION I ATE IT AS QUICKLY AS I COULD.

A-HO!

THAT WILL GIVE YOU A *WARRIOR'S HEART*, J.T.!

I DON'T LIKE THIS!

49

STOICISM? MY DAD ONCE TOLD ME I COULD TALK TO HIM ABOUT *ANYTHING.* I IMMEDIATELY TOLD HIM THAT SOME OF THE THINGS HE SAID HURT MY *FEELINGS.*

CLEARLY THE "MAN" INGREDIENT WAS SOMETHING I JUST DIDN'T HAVE, AND I HID DEEP DOWN THE ABSTRACT FEAR THAT I SIMPLY WOULD NEVER MEASURE *UP.*

...YOU'RE TOO SENSITIVE, INDIO.

MAYBE YOU SHOULD SAVE THAT KIND OF TALK FOR THE *WOMEN.*

GO LONG!

OH GOD, PLEASE DON'T LET ME MISS THIS AND BE A FAILURE!

THE FEAR OF BEING CONSIDERED A *WIMP* OR A *SISSY* WAS THE DRIVING FORCE BEHIND MOST OF THE MEAN THINGS I DID. IF THE FOCUS WASN'T ON *ME* ~ THAT WAS GOOD.

HUFF HUFF HUFF HUFF

NO WAY, LARD ASS!

PANT PANT WHEEZE

OH MAN IF HE OUTRUNS ME I'LL BE A *LAUGHINGSTOCK*- I'LL NEVER LIVE IT DOWN!

THAT'S WHAT LISTENING TO THE MEN TAUGHT ME. MY *MOTHER* DIDN'T THINK DIFFERENCE WAS WEAK.

MOM, I DON'T WANT TO PLAY WITH HIM, HE'S A RETARD—

SHAME ON YOU!

SMAK

YOU DON'T TALK THAT WAY ABOUT PEOPLE!

MOM, WHY DOES THAT GUY ACT THAT WAY?

HE'S JUST *GAY,* HONEY. HE'S ATTRACTED TO MEN INSTEAD OF *WOMEN.*

GROSS!

OH, STOP TALKING LIKE YOUR *FATHER.* WHEN WE LIVED IN *L.A.* IT WAS MY *GAY* FRIENDS WHO HELPED ME RAISE YOU WHEN HE WAS ON THE ROAD.

HUH.

I MISS THEM.

I THINK I ALWAYS REALIZED THAT MY FATHER WAS A *COMPLICATED MAN*, THAT HE SUFFERED THE SAME MANIC *UPS* AND *DOWNS* THAT I DID. THE SAME HOT TEMPER.

IT TOOK ME A *VERY LONG* TIME TO UNDERSTAND THAT PERHAPS HE SAW THOSE THINGS IN ME, AND THAT WHAT I THOUGHT OF AS *DISAPPOINTMENT* MAY HAVE BEEN *CONCERN* OR *MELANCHOLY.*

I'LL NEVER KNOW, BECAUSE MEN DON'T TALK ABOUT SUCH THINGS.

YET IN THE *MIDST* OF THE *UNPREDICTABILITY*
AND *DRUNKEN WEIRDNESS* WAS *SANCTUARY*.

GRANDMA AND
GRANDPA!

GRANDMA AND GRANDPA *TERRY* COULD *ALWAYS*
BE COUNTED ON. THEY'D *FOUGHT* FOR US.

HA HA!

WHENEVER POP HAD A *NIGHT GIG* WE WENT TO THEIR APARTMENT AND THEY *SPOILED*
US WITH KINDNESS, LOVE AND *STABILITY*. WITHIN THE CHAOTIC SWIRL-*STRUCTURE*.
CALM. CALM. CALM.
GRANDMA *COOKED* AND GRANDPA *CLEANED* AND WE'D GET A BOWL OF *BUTTER
PECAN ICE CREAM*. GRANDMA DRANK ANOTHER MARTINI AND WOULD HIT THE HAY.

AFTER, IT WAS *TV*
TIME WITH GRANDPA.

THE "UNTOUCHABLES", "THE
HONEYMOONERS" AND
THEN "SANFORD & SON."

WHEN THOSE "M·A·S·H"
HELICOPTERS CAME ON
IT WAS TIME FOR BED.

HOW COMFORTING
IT ALL WAS.

THEY LAUGHED AT EVERYTHING
WE DID SO WE ACTED SILLIER
TO MAKE THEM LAUGH MORE.

I MENTIONED ONCE THAT I
LOVED *COOL RANCH DORITOS*
AND AFTER THAT THERE WAS
ALWAYS A BAG IN THEIR HOME.

LITTLE GESTURES.

THEY, WHO HAD LOST THREE
OF THEIR FOUR SONS, TREATED
US LIKE *UNEXPECTED TREASURES*.

MOST SUNDAYS POP WORKED THE *WILLOWBROOK BALLROOM* - WHICH HE WASN'T *CRAZY* ABOUT. "BORING WALTZES FOR A BUNCH OF *OLD FOLKS*." HE'D DROP US OFF AT GRANDMA AND GRANDPA'S AND WE'D PLAY OUTSIDE UNTIL WE HEARD GRANDPA'S WHISTLE.

SOMETIMES GRANDMA WOULD HAVE TOO MANY *MARTINIS* AND GET A BIT *NASTY* BUT GRANDPA WOULD JUST LAUGH IT OFF. HE *SAW* HOW *SENSITIVE* I WAS AND WOULD SAY —

SOME SUNDAYS POP WOULD DROP US OFF AT A CHURCH, BUT WOULD NOT ATTEND WITH US.

DAD, WHY DO WE HAVE TO GO BUT YOU DON'T?

HEY- YEAH DAD, WHY?

IT'S NOT MY THING... OKAY YOU DON'T WANNA GO? FINE!

DON'T GO! SEE IF I CARE!

MOM WAS ALSO RAISED *CATHOLIC* AND HAD HORROR STORIES ABOUT HOW THE NUNS TREATED NATIVES.

DON DIDN'T LIKE RELIGION *PERIOD*. HE'D WATCH SUNDAY MORNING *TELEVANGELISTS* AS ENTERTAINMENT, ENLISTING US TO JOIN IN THE FUN DESPITE MOM'S *PROTESTS*.

OKAY, JIM - PUT YOUR HAND ON THE TV AND FEEL THE POWER OF *JAYZUSS*! HEAL! HEAL THE BOY! HEE-ULL!

DONALD STOP MAKING FUN!

HA HA HA!

I...I FEEL IT! THE HEALING!

KUNIKA WAS TAKEN AS A CHILD AND PUT IN A *CATHOLIC SCHOOL*, WHICH WAS COMMON PRACTICE. FORCIBLY REMOVE THE NATIVE CHILD - CUT OFF THEIR HAIR, GIVE THEM *CHRISTIAN* NAMES AND TORTURE THEM IF THEY SPOKE THEIR NATIVE LANGUAGE.

KILL THE INDIAN, SAVE THE MAN.

GEN. RICHARD H. PRATT. FOUNDER OF THE INFLUENTIAL CARLISLE INDIAN INDUSTRIAL SCHOOL

WHEN A PERSUASIVE *JEHOVAH'S WITNESS* CAME TO OUR DOOR, ELENA AND I DEDUCED SOMEONE COMING TO *US* WAS EASIER THAN GOING TO *CHURCH*.

SO WHY DON'T YOU GUYS WEAR CROSSES?

WELL, IF SOMEONE KILLED YOUR PARENTS WITH A *SHOTGUN*, WOULD YOU WEAR A TINY SHOTGUN AROUND YOUR NECK?

!

MOMMY...

IT DIDN'T LAST LONG. AFTER THAT WE WERE OFF THE *RELIGION* HOOK - INCLUDING OUR OWN NATIVE ONE.

"GEORGE OF THE JUNGLE?"

YES. THANK GOD.

SUNDAY NIGHTS WERE ALSO FOR DREAD AND *TERROR* AS I RARELY DID *HOMEWORK*.

YOU'RE GONNA DIE TOMORROW...

TIC TIC TIC TIC TIC TIC

SCHOOL ITSELF WAS A MIX, I HAD GOOD FRIENDS BUT THERE WERE BULLIES EVERYWHERE.

WHAT'RE YOU LOOKIN' AT, HOMO?

I'M JUST WALKIN' DOWN THE HALL!

?

J.T. DID YOU SEE SVENGOOLI SATURDAY?

WE TALKED CONSTANTLY ABOUT GIRLS AND "STAR WARS" BUT ONE WAS AN ABSOLUTE MYSTERY.

ER, CHRISTINE, DO YOU WANNA SEE SOMETHING FUNNY?

WHAT, YOUR FACE?

THERE'S NO COMING BACK FROM THAT ONE!

BEING A GENUINE *NERD* TRANSCENDED RACE BUT PUT A UNIVERSAL TARGET ON ONE'S BACK.

I HAVE A THEORY THAT *LUKE* IS GONNA PUSH THOSE BUTTONS ON VADER'S CHEST.

AND *THAT'S* HOW HE *KILLS HIM?!* HAHA, NO WAY.

WHY BOTHER TO BECOME A *JEDI* IF ALL - *OW!*

HEAD'S UP, NERD!

CLASS ITSELF WAS A HILARIOUSLY ONE-SIDED AFFAIR, ESPECIALLY HISTORY.

CHRISTOPHER COLUMBUS WAS A GREAT EXPLORER.

HE DISCOVERED THIS COUNTRY IN 1492 AND WAS, IN MANY WAYS, ONE OF THE FIRST AMERICANS.

AS FAR AS I *KNEW*, ELENA AND I WERE THE ONLY *NATIVES* IN OUR SCHOOL AND WE BOTH PLAYED IT DOWN IN THE INTEREST OF *SURVIVAL*.

THE *PILGRIMS* WERE PEACEFUL SETTLERS WHO FLED *EUROPE* SO THEY COULD PRACTICE THEIR RELIGION WITHOUT PERSECUTION.

PEW PEW

I TOOK IT IN, I MEMORIZED THE DATES AND DREW PICTURES OF THE MAYFLOWER.

THANKSGIVING IS A HOLIDAY OF PEACE AND SHARING. IT IS THE DAY THE PILGRIMS INVITED THE INDIANS TO SHARE IN THEIR BOUNTY.

THE **TRAGEDY** IS I BELIEVED IT ALL. WHY WOULD THEY **LIE**? I WASN'T TAUGHT ANYTHING DIFFERENT AT HOME, ON TV OR AT THE MOVIES.

ANDREW JACKSON WAS THE COMMON PEOPLE'S PRESIDENT.

IN FACT HE ONCE OPENED THE WHITE HOUSE AND INVITED ANYONE TO JUST DROP ON IN! IT WAS... QUITE A PARTY!

HA HA HA REALLY? AWESOME! DUDE! WHAT A COOL GUY!

ANDREW "INDIAN KILLER" JACKSON WAS ON **MONEY** NEXT TO GOD'S NAME. HIS INDIAN RELOCATION ACT WAS NEVER MENTIONED IN OUR TEXT AND THE TRAIL OF TEARS WAS A PARAGRAPH. A FOOTNOTE.

NOR A MENTION THAT THE PILGRIMS WERE CONSIDERED FANATICS BACK HOME AND WERE EATING BELTS, SHOES, AND POSSIBLY EACH OTHER BEFORE THE NATIVES STEPPED IN.

OR THAT COLUMBUS CHOPPED THE HANDS OFF NATIVES WHEN THEY COULD NOT SUPPLY HIM WITH THE GOLD HE WAS CONVINCED THEY HAD ~

~ HE DID NOT REALIZE THAT ALMOST ALL THE GOLD HE SAW WAS GOLD THE NATIVES FOUND ON THE SHORES, WASHED UP FROM SUNKEN SPANISH SHIPS. *

*I'D READ THIS ALL LATER, AFTER I WAS ALLOWED TO DEVELOP A MIND OF MY OWN.

57

OVER THE CREEK BEHIND THE HOUSE HUNG A ROPE, THE END OF IT BURNT TO A GUMMY STUMP.

MY PAL STEVE AND I WERE INDIANA JONES, SWINGING ACROSS, WHEN A COUPLE BURNOUTS EMERGED FROM THE FOLIAGE.

WHAT'RE YOU FAGGOTS DOING?

GULP.

EVERYONE KNEW TO STAY AWAY FROM THESE GUYS BUT STEVE KNEW THEM THROUGH HIS BROTHER AND WAS UNAFRAID.

"WE'RE JUST FUCKIN' SWINGIN' BACK AND FORTH," HE SAID.

THE BIG ONE POINTED AT ME. "THE FUCK'RE YOU? MEXICAN?"

"I'M INDIAN."

HE STEPPED CLOSER. "I DON'T FUCKIN' LIKE INDIANS."

"HE'S HALF IRISH." STEVE SAID.

BIG BOY THOUGHT ABOUT IT, SPIT. "HE GETS A PASS THIS TIME."

...YEARS LATER I'D GET TO KNOW BIG BOY AS THE BONEHEAD HE WAS. IN HIS HEART WAS VERY LITTLE TRUE MALICE, NOR IN HIS HEAD MANY ORIGINAL THOUGHTS.

ALL HIS ATTITUDES WERE TAUGHT TO HIM. ODDLY ENOUGH I WOULD GROW TO LIKE HIM A LOT, BUT I ALWAYS KEPT A DISTANCE.

WHAT DID "INDIAN" MEAN TO THE AVERAGE AMERICAN, THOUGH? I WAS TAUGHT THAT THEY WERE MOSTLY ENEMIES OR SIDEKICKS.

ACCORDING TO MOVIES AND TV THEY WERE ALWAYS KILLING INNOCENT WHITE PEOPLE FOR NO GOOD REASON. NO REASONING WITH A SAVAGE.

SO WHEN THE WHITE HERO CONFRONTED THEM THERE WAS NATURALLY NO SOLUTION BUT DEATH.

WELL I'M JUST... GONNA HAFTA... GO 'N GET HER BACK.

THEY WERE SO STUPID AND SAVAGE, IN FACT, THAT KILLING THEM WAS EASY. THE BLUE-EYED ITALIANS THEY HIRED TO PORTRAY NATIVES JUST SCREAMED AND RODE THEIR HORSES INTO RIFLE RANGE. CAN'T BLAME LAZY WRITERS FOR USING A CONVENIENT DEVICE.

THOSE REDSKINS 'R CHARGIN'! HOLD 'EM OFF, FELLAS!

WOO WOO WOO WOO YEEHEE WOO— HEYA HEYA WOO

KEEP THE WOMEN HID!

BANG BANG

BANG

IMPLIED RAPE AND TORTURE SEEMED TO AWAIT ANYONE UNFORTUNATE ENOUGH TO BE CAPTURED ALIVE.

SAVE THE LAST BULLET FOR YOURSELF. YOU DON'T WANT TO BE TAKEN.

OCCASIONALLY THE HERO, WHO WAS PROTECTING THE SETTLERS AND THEIR RIGHT TO SAY "THIS IS MINE NOW, GET OVER IT," WOULD HAVE A BEGRUDGING RESPECT FOR HIS RED ENEMY.

HE WAS... ONE HELL OF AN ADVERSARY.

I NEVER HEARD HIM SAY—

AND HE WAS KILLED TRYING TO PROTECT HIS FAMILY FROM US.

I BURIED MYSELF IN COMICS, MOVIES, AND BOOKS.

I DIDN'T DREAM OF BEING GERONIMO - I DIDN'T KNOW HIM AS THE UNCOMPROMISING TACTICAL GENIUS WHO EVADED THE U.S. ARMY FOR YEARS - I KNEW HIM AS WHAT WHITE GUYS JOKINGLY YELLED WHEN THEY HAD TO JUMP OUT OF SOMETHING.

MY DAD THOUGHT INDIANS OF OLD WERE ABOUT THE WISEST AND TOUGHEST PEOPLE THAT EVER LIVED. WHEN I TOLD MY MOM THAT HE USED TO DREAM HE WAS INDIAN (WHICH HE INDEED SAID TO ME) SHE CHUCKLED AND ROLLED HER EYES.

"OF COURSE HE DID, HE WAS A BOY."

MOM - ESPECIALLY DRUNK - WOULD ACT AS THOUGH BEING NATIVE WAS THE HARDEST THING THAT COULD HAPPEN TO SOMEONE. THAT SORROW AND TRAUMA RAN IN OUR VEINS, GENERATIONAL WOUNDS SO DEEP THAT ONE DIDN'T DETECT IT UNTIL LIFE CRUSHED THEM.

YET SHE LAUGHED MORE THAN ANYONE I'VE EVER KNOWN AND ALWAYS HAMMERED HOME THAT THE INDIAN WAY WAS DIFFERENT. BE GOOD TO EVERYONE. HELP. BE GOOD. I DON'T KNOW IF THAT'S THE "INDIAN WAY" OR NOT BUT I THINK IT WAS HER WAY.

SHE DIDN'T TEACH ME ABOUT GERONIMO, CHEWIE, AND I DIDN'T GROW UP WITH OTHER NATIVES.

I GREW UP WITH MOVIES.

KINDA HID THAT I WAS NATIVE.

UNLESS I WAS IN THE DELLS, OF COURSE. THEN I COULD RELAX.

SORT OF.

WITH THE CUSTODY ARRANGEMENT WE'D SPEND *TWO* SUMMER WEEKS AT A TIME WITH *EACH PARENT.* SOMETIMES WE'D SPEND THE WHOLE SUMMER IN THE *DELLS.* LATER WE WERE TOLD IT WAS SO THEY COULD ALL DRINK WITHOUT US AROUND.

AT SOME POINT *ELENA* BEGAN GOING OFF WITH KUNIKA MORE AND I'D DISAPPEAR ON MY *BIKE.*

WE DIDN'T CARE WHY.

J.T. & ELENA!

WHERE IS EVERYONE? LET'S PLAY!

BARK BARK

HEADING INTO THE WASTELAND FOR PRECIOUS GUZZOLINE!

IF SHE WASN'T DOING THINGS WITH KUNIKA SHE WAS OFF WITH *CHOKA* SOMEWHERE. *LEARNING.*

WHAT ARE THESE FOR, CHOKA?

THOSE ARE GOOD IF YOU HAVE A STOMACH ACHE.

JUST CHEW THEM. YOU CAN FIND THEM RIGHT OFF THE ROAD.

OVER IN THAT THICKET IS—

HOLY SMOKERS! LOOK AT THAT EAGLE, ELENA!

IT'S GOOD MEDICINE, JUST *SEEING* ONE OF THEM.

WOW.

I SPENT THOSE DAYS *SWIMMING* AND PLAYING *DEADLY DISCS OF TRON* AT THE *STAND ROCK INDIAN CEREMONIAL GROUNDS.*

SOMETIMES WE KIDS WATCHED *MOVIES* ALL DAY. I THINK I SAW *"NIGHTMARE ON ELM STREET 2"* ABOUT TWENTY TIMES. SAW *"ZAPPED"* TWICE THAT.

PEPPERONI PIZZA AND AN ORANGE POP, PLEASE.

YOU SHOULD TRY EATING SOMETHING GREEN ONCE IN A WHILE, J.T.

JEEEEZ.

FOOD

GAMES

I'M *HUNGRY.* IS THERE ANYTHING TO EAT?

JUST THAT COMMODITY CHEESE... BUT IT'S ALL HARD AND BROWN, IT'LL GIVE YOU THE RUNS.

HE HAS THE RUNS ANYWAY THOUGH, AYY.

HELP YOURSELF, FUCKER-

WHEN THE TREES GREW *DARK* I'D HEAD BACK TO *KUNIKA'S* TO GET READY FOR THE *NIGHT.*

EVERYONE IN THE HEIGHTS SEEMED TO BE GETTING READY TO GO TO THE *SAME PLACE.*

I DO HAVE THE RUNS.

YOU'RE GONNA BE *LATE.*

JUST GOTTA USE THE JOHN. SEE YOU THERE.

JEEEZ

HEY, TEGA!

AHO!

THAT BIKE IS TOO BIG FOR YOU, J.T.!

OK!

HUFF HUFF HUFF

THIS WAY TO STAND ROCK INDIAN CEREMONIAL

SQUEEK SQUEEK

DOWN THE BACK ROAD THROUGH THE WOODS
AS THE WORLD TURNED *BLUE*, THEN *BLACK*.

MOSQUITOES BUZZED MY EARS AGAINST THE SOFT
TUNING OF THE *DRUM* – UNEVEN, QUICK, THEN SILENT.

THE MAGIC SOUND OF *JINGLE DANCERS* WALKING
OR FIXING THEIR *LEGGINGS*, LIKE GENTLE *RAIN*.

WOODSMOKE – AN ELEMENTAL SMELL, MIXED
WITH *PINE* AND *POPCORN*. THE ABSURD THRILL
OF BEING *BEHIND THE SCENES*. *MAGIC*.

BUT I WASN'T PART OF IT. I WAS ONLY A *WITNESS* TO IT AS I PASSED *THROUGH* – AN
OBSERVER OF A FAMILYHOOD THAT WENT ON, *INDIFFERENT*, AS I GLIDED
THROUGH LIKE A SHADOW. *MY JOB WAS NOT WITH MY BROTHERS AND SISTERS.*

I SOLD SOUVENIR BOOKS AT THE STAND ROCK INDIAN CEREMONIAL.

A NATURAL AMPITHEATRE, TOURISTS COULD ENJOY NATIVES PERFORMING TRADITIONAL DANCES.

MY TEGA *LANCE* WOULD EMCEE, MAKING THE AUDIENCE ROAR WITH DRY HUMOR OR HUSHING THEM WITH SOLEMN SINCERITY.

THE DANCES WERE GENUINE.

AND IT SEEMED EVERYONE IN THE HEIGHTS WORKED AT "THE ROCK."

I WAS A *HAM* AND WAS PUT TO WORK ON THE *FRONT END.* I NEVER DANCED.

SOOOVENEER BOOKS! GET 'EM WHILE THEY'RE HOT! LIMITED TIME!

HOW CUTE! I'LL TAKE ONE, YOUNG MAN.

MOM EVEN WORKED THERE FOR A WHILE. SHE'D APPEAR ON THE *BLUFF WALL,* BEAUTIFUL AND DISTANT, AND SING "INDIAN LOVE CALL" WHILE I WAVED, TRYING TO GET HER TO SEE ME.

SHE LOOKED LIKE A PAINTING.

AT THE FINALE A MASSIVE U.S. FLAG WAS UNFURLED AND EVERYONE STOOD AND SALUTED, I SUPPOSE TO LET THE AUDIENCE KNOW THERE WERE NO HARD FEELINGS AND THAT THEY WERE STILL IN AMERICA.

I WAS USUALLY BUMMING AROUND THE GIFT SHOP BY THEN, WITH THE PLASTIC *TOMAHAWKS* AND CHEAP *HEADDRESSES*. IT HAD THE SAME PLASTIC AND CEDAR SMELL EVERY "NATIVE GIFT SHOP" SEEMS TO.

SELL A LOT OF THEM SOOVENEER BOOKS, J.T.?

YUP.

I'D PUT OFF THE LONELY BIKE RIDE HOME AS LONG AS *POSSIBLE*, I WAS TERRIFIED OF THE DARK WOODS. EVERY EVIL SPIRIT, EVERY *HOMPOOK*... THEY WERE *WAITING*.

JUST DON'T... SHOW... **FEAR!**

THE ONLY STREETLIGHT WAS HALFWAY TO KUNIKA'S AND I'D PAUSE THERE, HEARING THE DISTANT DRUMS FROM THE CEREMONIAL. A GOOD SOUND.

HA HA, JIM— YOU FOOL.

OH GOD. YOU JERK. YOU'RE ONLY HALFWAY HOME!

65

EVERYWHERE WERE
THE TREES
IN THE TREES, SHADOWS
IN THE SHADOWS, SPIRITS

THE SPIRIT WORLD WAS
EVERYWHERE TOO—
BUT FELT STRONGEST
IN THE WOODS

SILENT, DEEP, A MYSTERY
FILLED WITH SECRETS
ANCIENT KNOWLEDGE

ANIMALS, BIRDS—MIGHT NOT
BE WHAT THEY SEEM

IN DAYLIGHT THE TREES WERE
BEAUTIFUL, SACRED
SILENT LIFEGIVERS

IN NIGHT'S SHADOW THEY BECAME
WHISPERING, SWAYING
SENTINELS OF THE UNKNOWN.

ALL SHADOWS FADED UNDER THE SUMMER SUN.

HOT DOGS WERE PURE *BLISS* AFTER A SWIM, EVEN *BOLOGNA SANDWICHES* TASTED LIKE HEAVEN.

THE BEACH WAS LITTERED WITH TREE BRANCHES AND PEPPERED WITH *COOL* PATCHES OF SHADOW.

THE WATER WAS *ALWAYS* COLD.

GOING DOWN TO THE *RIVER* AT STAND ROCK PIER WAS THE *GREATEST*.

IT WAS A TEN-MINUTE WALK FROM *KUNIKA'S* AND ALWAYS DESERTED.

WE'D CLIMB A HIDDEN PATH TO THE *BLUFF* AND WAIT FOR THE TOUR *BOATS* TO COME ALONG, THEN *LEAP* FROM THE TOP OF THE *ROCKS*.

THEN SOMEONE GOT *SCABIES* SWIMMING THERE AND WE WENT BACK TO MOVIES AND *COMMODITY CHEESE*.

!

CLAP
CLAP
CLAP

THERE ONCE WAS AN OLD GRAY DOG THAT WANDERED THE NEIGHBORHOOD, GENTLE AND KNOWING. THE ELDERS SPOKE TO HIM AS ONE OF THEIR OWN AND HIS SAD, INTELLIGENT EYES UNDERSTOOD.

THE CHILDREN JUMPED ON HIS ANCIENT BACK AND HE CRUMPLED BENEATH THEM UNTIL THEY RAN OFF, THEN ROSE AND QUIETLY PADDED AWAY.

HE JOINED ME ONE DAY AS I WAS WALKING ALONG THE HIGHWAY. I HONESTLY FELT HONORED THAT HE CHOSE TO KEEP ME COMPANY AND TALKED TO HIM THE WAY I'D SEEN MY GRANDMOTHER DO.

HE'D RUN TO THE WOODS WITH NO WARNING... AND THEN A CAR WOULD WHIZ BY.

ONCE THE CAR WAS GONE HE'D RETURN TO MY SIDE AND I'D TALK TO HIM A LITTLE BIT MORE.

THAT IS WHY, WHEN I HEARD HE'D BEEN KILLED BY A CAR, I KNEW IT WAS ON PURPOSE.

THAT PUP WAS A SPIRIT, I SINCERELY BELIEVE!... AND SOME BASTARD KILLED HIM FOR MALICE OR FUN.

MAYBE THAT DAY MAGIC DIED FOR ME A LITTLE AS WELL.

WHERE ARE YOU GOING, MY FRIEND?

YOU ARE SPECIAL FRIEND.

HOW'D YOU KNOW THAT CAR WAS COMING?

THE LAST SUMMER I WORKED AT "THE ROCK" WAS AS A PARKING LOT ATTENDANT. MY COUSIN AND I DIRECTED CARS WHILE BULLSHITTING ABOUT MUSIC, GIRLS, AND DRINKING. I STUCK TO MUSIC. I KNEW NOTHING ABOUT GIRLS AND SWORE NEVER TO DRINK.

THATS ALL OLD PEOPLE MUSIC. HAVE YOU EVEN HEARD VAN HALEN?

YEAH. BUT I LIKE PINK FLOYD.

TCH. LAME.

SO WHEN'RE YOU GONNA GO BUZZIN' WITH US?

I TOLD YOU, NEVER. I'M NOT GONNA BE LIKE OUR PARENTS.

FINE THEN. JUST THERE'LL BE GIRLS THERE TOO IS ALL.

SO MY MOM TAPED "TERMINATOR," WANNA WATCH IT LATER?

YEAH. WHAT GIRLS GO THERE, ANYWAY?

COME WITH. FIND OUT.

THAT NIGHT I SNUCK OUT WITH ANOTHER COUSIN WHO KNEW WHERE "CANCER HILL" WAS. FEAR AND EXCITEMENT, JOY AND DREAD, TOOK TURNS FLIPPING MY STOMACH.

WHAT WAS THAT?

JEEEZ, NOTHIN! OKAY, I HEAR THEM.

WHO'S GONNA BE THERE?

JASON VOORHEES. I DUNNO, OKAY? CALM DOWN ALREADY.

IT WAS A REVELATION. EVERYONE I WAS AFRAID OF OR THOUGHT DIDN'T LIKE ME... WERE ALL CHEERING MY PRESENCE. THE TENSION LEFT BUT THE DREAD WAS STRONG.

J.T.!

WONDRIN' WHEN YOU'D FIND YER WAY OUT HERE, SON.

HEY BROTHER.

HI.

AHO!

GIMME A BEER.

BEER

THE DESIRE TO **BELONG** WAS POWERFUL. ALL IT'D TAKE WAS ACCEPTING A BEER. ALL I NEEDED TO DO.

JEEZ, REALLY FISHIN' AROUND IN THERE AYYY. HEY GRAB ME ONE TOO.

WANT A COLD ONE, JIMMY T.?

MUUMUMM...

YES? IS THERE A PROBLEM, JIM?

BUT EVERYTHING I'D SEEN TOLD ME IT WAS THE WORST KIND OF **POISON**, THE KIND YOU COULDN'T STOP USING. I'D SWORN NEVER TO BE LIKE THEM.

EARTH TO J.T.—YOU WANT A BEER OR WHAT?

I....

C'MON YOU LITTLE SISSY.

WHO KNOWS WHAT WAS SAID? WHAT I **HEARD** WAS:

TCH. JEEZ, HE AIN'T ONE OF US ANYWAY.

YEAH, I'LL HAVE ONE OF THOSE.

THAT NIGHT I ACTED A **FOOL** AND I **LOVED** IT. I TEASED MY COUSIN AND EVERYONE **LAUGHED**. I FLOATED **OUTSIDE** OF MYSELF.

THE NEXT DAY I WAS **SICK** AS A DOG AND EVERYONE SEEMED TO **KNOW** BUT DID NOT SEEM TO **CARE**.

WELL... LOOKS LIKE **SOMEONE** WAS OUT LATE LAST NIGHT.

!

ONCE I REALIZED IT WAS ALMOST EXPECTED, I WANTED **NOTHING** MORE THAN TO GO BACK TO "C" HILL AGAIN. TO **DRINK** AGAIN.

OF COURSE I WANNA WATCH "TIME BANDITS." BUT... YOU GOING BACK TO "C" HILL TOMORROW?

I DUNNO. PROBABLY.

WELL... LEMME KNOW.

I FELT **SAFE** THERE, **LOVED** AND A PART OF SOMETHING. A **BOND**, AND I WANTED TO BUZZ FOREVER.

IT'S THE "C" HILL RAP! YO YO YO! GEORGE-BEAT BOX, SUCKA!

BFFF-PFAW-HA-HAW

EVEN THE AWFUL **SICKNESS** WAS JUST **PART** OF THAT BOND.

HOOOOO! MAN DOWN. HA HA AYY.

HOO-WA!

SOMEONE'S DOWN FER THE COUNT.

YER BABAS ARE DOWN FOR THE COUNT AYYYYY.

NO, I... GOT THIS—

BLUH

YOU BETTER NOT WAKE UP KUNIKA J.T... I'M SHERIOUS.

JEEEEZ I WON'T.

WHAT HE ALWAYS SEZ, ENIT?

72

BEFORE LONG IT WAS ALL I REALLY THOUGHT ABOUT, AND I BECAME A COLOSSAL PEST.

YEAH, SO THEN SHE COMES ALONG AND—*WHAT, J.T.?*

NOTHIN'... JUST ARE YOU GOIN' *"BUZZIN"* LATER?

MAYBE, OKAY? JEEZ!

ANYWAYS—

WELL LEMME KNOW.

THE NIGHT NO LONGER MEANT *FEAR OF SPIRITS* OR THE *THRILL OF THE SHOW*.... IT NOW MEANT THE CHANCE TO *SNEAK OUT* AND *DRINK*. I TRIED TO HIDE IT FROM *ELENA* BUT SHE SAW WHAT WAS HAPPENING.

YOU THREE SHOULD TRY STAYING *IN* FOR A NIGHT.

YEAH OKAY MA... WE WERE JUST GONNA WATCH *"ZAPPED"* AGAIN ANYWAY TONIGHT, ENIT.

YUP.

I KNEW, EVERY STEP OF THE WAY, THAT BOOZING WAS A *BAD PATH*—I JUST DIDN'T *CARE* ANYMORE. THAT DIDN'T MEAN I WANTED ELENA TO SEE ME DRINKING, THE *THOUGHT* OF THAT FILLED ME WITH *GUILT* AND *SHAME*.

THE COMMUNITY WAS *ALREADY* SMALL ENOUGH.

WELL LOOK AT THIS. *JIMMY T.* SAY IT FOR YOUR *TEGA*. SAY *"D'LIN D'LIN HEIGHTS"* FOR ME.

OH GOD HE'S HERE? TIME TO GO!

SOME OF THOSE GUYS *SCARED* ME AND THEY ALL THOUGHT THEY WERE MY *TEGA*. MEN WITH AN AURA OF *DANGER*, AND NOT THE *"COOL"* KIND. *HAUNTED* MEN, *BROKEN* MEN, *ANGRY* MEN WITH WARRIOR SPIRITS *GONE TWISTED* WITH *IMPOTENT RAGE* AND *SOURED* BY BOOZE.

MEN WHO, IN A DIFFERENT TIME, MIGHT HAVE BEEN LEADERS OF PEOPLE.

WARRIORS. HUNTERS. PROVIDERS. DEFENDERS. CHIEFS. STORYTELLERS.

BUT THEY LIVED *NOW*, IN *THIS* WORLD, AND IT SEEMED TO *CRUSH* THEM.

BOOZE MADE ME *MAUDLIN* AND EVEN *MORE* EMOTIONAL THAN I ALREADY *WAS*, WHICH LED TO MANY AWKWARD OUTBURSTS AND *CONFESSIONS* - WHICH WERE ACCEPTED WITHOUT *COMMENT, QUESTION,* OR *JUDGMENT.*

WHY DO THEY DO THOSE THINGS... DON'T THEY LOVE US AT ALL?

THEY'RE FUCKED UP TOO, BRO... BUT WE'RE NOT LIKE THEM. WE'LL *NEVER* BE LIKE THEM.

I KNOW I'M NOT. GONNA GET THE HELL OUTTA HERE 'FORE THAT HAPPENS...

IT WAS PROFOUND *RELIEF.* SOMETHING INSIDE ME'D BEEN TIGHTENING LIKE A *DRUM* AND WAS SUDDENLY *SPRUNG. I* COULD BREATHE. I COULD FLY.

FUCK YOU, PARENTS!

HEY SCHOOL, WHY DON'T YOU FUCK OFF TOO?

THINK I FEAR YOU, *SPIRITS?* WELL SURPRISE... FUCK YOU!

WANNA FIGHT ME? I DON'T CARE HOW BIG YOU ARE!

HOMPOOK... WHERE YOU AT, BITCH?

I DON'T CARE!!

NUCLEAR WAR?? WHO GIVES A SHIT!

I DON'T CARE!

WHEN SCHOOL STARTED ALL THAT ABRUPTLY ENDED, THOUGH I'D OCCASIONALLY STEAL FROM DON.

JUST A COUPLE CANS BUT IT TAKES THE EDGE OFF.

FEELS FUNNY, KIND OF POINTLESS TO DRINK THESE BY MYSELF. OH WELL...

WHEN WE WENT UP TO THE DELLS FOR CHRISTMAS I SPLIT AS SOON AS I COULD, RACING OFF WITH MY COUSINS TO MAKE UP FOR LOST DRINKING TIME.

JEEZ, SLOW DOWN, J.T.!

HOOO.... IT'S NOT A RACE, DICK TRICKLE! PACE YOURSELF!

GLUG GLUG NO.

I BLACKED OUT FOR THE FIRST TIME.

AT SOME POINT I VOMITED ON KUNIKA'S BED. THE CONSEQUENCE FLOODGATE OPENED.

OH DONALD... WHAT DO WE DO? MY SON—

LET HIM BE SICK, DEBBIE!

ALL OVER MY COMFORTER!

AND SICK I WAS. FOR SEVERAL AWFUL DAYS.

NOT HUNGRY, JIM? WOULD YOU PREFER SOME OF YOUR NEW SISTER'S BABY FOOD?

NO.

DONALD...

IT WAS NOTHING COMPARED TO WHAT MY BRAIN WAS DOING TO ME. I'D LET EVERYONE DOWN.

I'D LET MYSELF DOWN. I WAS NO DIFFERENT FROM THEM. NO BETTER.

JUST ANOTHER DRUNK

THE **GUILT** WAS **BEYOND PROFOUND**, ESPECIALLY WITH **POP**. HE'D LOST HIS **LICENSE** TO DRINKING AND WAS BUMMING RIDES TO **GIGS**. HE GOT **SOBER**.

HEY, KIDS.

AND HE **STAYED** SOBER. HE DIDN'T EVEN **KICK** MY **ASS** WHEN HE HEARD, WHICH I'D BEEN READY FOR. HE JUST SEEEMED **SAD**...AND THAT WAS **WORSE**.

DAD...I'M SORRY.

HE'D EVEN PAID ATTENTION WHEN I'D MENTIONED WANTING TO **SKATEBOARD** AND GOT ME ONE FOR **CHRISTMAS**. IT WAS AN **UNUSUAL MOVE**.

I'M NOT...WORTHY OF THIS LOVE...

WHEN THE SICKNESS FINALLY SUBSIDED I HAD A **NEW RESOLVE**. **NEVER AGAIN**, NO MATTER WHAT.

NEVER AGAIN.

PART 2

I STAYED AT KONIKA'S IN THE *HEIGHTS* BUT SPENT MORE TIME ALONE. THERE WAS ALWAYS PLENTY OF *DRAMATIC GOINGS-ON* BUT I WAS TOO BUSY READING *FANGORIA*, LISTENING TO THE *WHO*, AND DAYDREAMING ABOUT *GIRLS*.

GOT A FEELING TWENTY-ONE IS GONNA BE A GOOD YEAR...

HOW LONG HAVE THEY BEEN GONE?

NOBODY'S SEEN 'EM SINCE THEY LEFT THE BAR. HE WAS DRIVING, TOO. JEEZ.

HE'S GOING TO END UP IN JAIL AGAIN. YOU JUST WATCH.

I FELL IN LOVE 483 TIMES A DAY BUT I COULDN'T FIGURE WHAT I WAS DOING WRONG.

SO I DREW AND READ AND DAYDREAMED.

I JUST DON'T GET IT!

LIKE, I'M SO SURE.

I KNOW, RIGHT?

FACE IT, CREEP.

YOU'RE NOT KURT RUSSELL. YOU'RE JUST A WEIRDO.

EMPLOYEE

STAND ROCK INDIAN EMONIA

THE MAGIC OF THE WOODS AND THE *HEIGHTS* BURNED AWAY THAT HOT SUMMER. I WORKED A JOB AND SO ALSO GONE WERE THE MIXED BLESSINGS OF CHILDHOOD.

HUFF HUFF HUFF

INDIAN HEIGHTS 2 MILES

SQUEEK SQUEEK

HORMONES, MY LOVE OF THE *WEIRD* AND *MACABRE*, AND MY VERY BEING IN GENERAL MADE ME FEEL DIFFERENT.

AS I GOT OLDER I BEGAN TO SEE FAMILY POLITICS. MY *MOTHER* WAS A *HOTBUTTON*. SHE LEFT. SHE WENT TO LIVE IN THE *WHITE WORLD*. SHE WAS ALWAYS *READING* AND THOUGHT SHE WAS BETTER **THAN**.

THE FACT THAT MY FATHER WAS *WHITE* AND THAT I WASN'T FROM THE *HEIGHTS* FELT MORE THAN EVER LIKE *DEFINING CHARACTERISTICS*.

I WAS NOT A "TOUGH GUY" AND WAS ABOUT AS *STOIC* AS *WET CARDBOARD*. EVERYONE WAS PLAYING *BASKETBALL* WHILE I READ "*DAREDEVIL*" AND RAY *BRADBURY*... I COULD NOT DO THE "*HARD INDIAN FACE*" WITHOUT BUSTING INTO A GIGGLE.

AND I WAS NO LONGER *DRINKING*, SO I WAS SIMPLY *LEFT OUT*.

WITHOUT COMPLAINT, I DRIFTED FROM IT ALL. IF THEY HAD A PROBLEM WITH ME OR DIDN'T THINK I *BELONGED*... WELL, GOODBYE.

SADLY IT WAS THE LAST SUMMER I SPENT UP THERE.

ELENA AND I RETURNED *HOME* - I'D BUMMED AROUND ALL *SUMMERLONG* AND SHE'D SPENT THE TIME *LEARNING FROM CHOKA* AND *KUNIKA*. I MANAGED TO EXPAND MY *"X-MEN"* COLLECTION.

I'D BEEN TO THE *SUNDANCE* IN SOUTH DAKOTA A FEW TIMES - *MUCH* OF THE FAMILY DROVE THERE FROM THE DELLS... IT WAS A *SACRED* THING AND *MYSTERIOUS* TO ME.

I RODE UP WITH *CHOKA* ONE YEAR AND HE TOLD ME ABOUT BEING *SHOT DOWN* AS A FIGHTER PILOT IN *WWII* BUT I JUST WATCHED HIM *PULL WHISKERS* FROM HIS FACE WITH A *COILED SPRING* AND TRIED NOT TO *PUKE* FROM HIS *SWISHER SWEET CIGAR* SMOKE.

JIM, I THINK I'M GOING TO *COMMIT* TO THE *SUNDANCE*.

OH YEAH? THAT'S GOOD, YOU *SHOULD!*

YOU EVER THINK OF GOING BACK TO IT?

UM... I DON'T REALLY FEEL PART OF ALL THAT.

MONTANA CHARLY'S FLEA MARKET

COMIX

A *LAME*, REBELLIOUS INDIFFERENCE EVENTUALLY TOOK HOLD. CONFUSION TURNED TO *FRUSTRATION*, *ANGER*, AND FINALLY *APATHY*. I JUST DID NOT UNDERSTAND THE CEREMONIES.

I DID WHAT WAS ASKED OF ME BUT ANY CHANCE I GOT WAS SPENT BUMMING AROUND.

MEANWHILE, *ELENA* WAS FINDING HER PATH.

JIM, THEY'RE GONNA DO A *SWEAT* TONIGHT IF YOU WANT TO GO PRAY...

UH... AM I SUPPOSED TO?

YOU HAVEN'T SEEN *"EVIL DEAD 2"* YET? OH MY GOD. THE CAMERAWORK ALONE IS WORTH THE RENTAL!

YOU BEEN *LAID* YET, J.T.?

UH... YEAH?

EVENTUALLY I'D WANDER OFF *ALONE* WITH MY SKETCHBOOK. EVERYONE SEEMED TO KNOW EACH OTHER AND I WAS JUST A *STRANGER*.

NOBODY WILL EVEN NOTICE I'M NOT THERE.

I GUESS I NEEDED TO GET COMFORTABLE WITH FEELING LIKE AN OUTSIDER. IT WAS TIME FOR *HIGH SCHOOL.*

IT'LL BE FINE...

...JUST DON'T GET *NOTICED.*

HINSDALE SOUTH HIGH SCHOOL

WELC ME STUDENT

MY HIGH SCHOOL HAD KIDS FROM OBSCENELY WEALTHY HOMES, MIDDLE CLASS FAMILIES, AND THE NEIGHBORHOOD *STEVE, DEAN,* AND *I* CAME FROM. NOT *DIRT POOR*—JUST POOR ENOUGH.

EVERYONE TESTED EVERYONE— I THINK WE WERE ALL AFRAID OF EACH OTHER BUT DIDN'T WANT TO *BACK DOWN.*

THE GROUP I HAD *LEAST* IN COMMON WITH WERE THE *JOCKS.* A FEW BECAME FRIENDS BUT ON THE WHOLE THEY MADE ME *NERVOUS.* THEY WERE BULLIES.

HA HA HA! HOMOS.

THESE FUCKIN' TURDS.

ASSHOLES.

WHAT'RE *YOU* LOOKING AT, PUSSY? I'LL FUCKIN' KILL YOU, DUDE.

KEEP WALKIN', DINGLE-BERRY.

THE BLAZE

WHO FARTED? KEVIN MATHEWS AM 1000

PUBERTY WAS KICKING IN WITH A VENGEANCE. MY HAIR WAS *GREASY* AND MY SKIN GOT OILY, SOON MY FACE WAS BREAKING OUT AND — HORROR OF HORRORS — SO WAS MY BACK. CHANGING IN THE **LOCKER** ROOM WAS A TEST OF *SPEED* AND *CONTORTION.*

DUDE, *FIVE BUCKS* SAYS I BANG HER FRIDAY AFTER THE GAME, DUDE.

YEAH!

YOU'RE ON, PUSSY!

OH GOD...

...SAFE AGAIN, FOR NOW.

I HATE EVERYONE.

I BECAME A **CLASS CLOWN** — THE ONLY WAY I THOUGHT GIRLS WOULD *NOTICE* ME.

OKAY, MR. TERRY. DOWN, BEFORE YOU HURT YOUR SELF.

DUDE!

SECRETLY I WONDERED IF I LOOKED "TOO INDIAN" AND THAT WAS WHY GIRLS DIDN'T NOTICE ME ~ THERE WAS NOTHING I COULD DO ABOUT THAT.

NOPE. YOU'RE JUST UGLY.

POP, OF COURSE, WAS A TREMENDOUS HELP DURING THIS DELICATE, INSECURE TIME.

I DON'T GET IT, MAN, WHEN I WAS YOUR AGE EVERYTHING WAS *ABOUT GIRLS*, NOT WEIRD BOOKS AND COMICS. ARE...ARE YOU A MARICÓN OR SOMETHING?

HUFF. NO, DAD.

I'M GOIN TO MY ROOM TO READ.

JIMMY, I KNOW YOU AIN'T A *MARICÓN* BUT WHAT GIVES?

NOTHIN'. I'LL TALK TO THE WOMEN ABOUT IT.

BAM!

84

I GREW QUEESY AS SHE EXPLAINED HOW THE MEDICATIONS WOULD AFFECT HER, THAT FATIGUE AND ILLNESS WOULD BE THE NORM.

I GREW RESENTFUL.

RESENTFUL AT WHAT I BEGAN TO SEE AS WEAKNESS.

SHE WAS SUPPOSED TO BE STRONG! SHE WAS SUPPOSED TO PROTECT US FROM THE BAD SHIT, NOT CONSTANTLY FALL VICTIM TO IT! MY MIND WENT TO DARK PLACES AS HER VOICE TRAILED OFF.

NIGHTS OF TERROR WHEN SHE AND DON GOT DRUNK AND THINGS WOULD TURN UGLY.

NOOOO!

NO PLEASE

WHIMPER

UNSUCCESSFULLY PLAYING THE CLOWN TO TRY AND PULL HER OUT OF THE BLACK MOODS.

MOM, LOOK!

MOM!

HEY MOM!

IGOR!

THE SUMMER SHE AND DON STAYED DRUNK AND MADE ELENA AND ME MOVE GRAVEL FROM ONE SIDE OF THE DRIVEWAY TO THE OTHER. IT FELT LIKE PUNISHMENT BUT IT WAS JUST TO KEEP US AWAY WHILE THEY BOOZED IT UP.

WHY DO WE HAVE TO DO THIS ALL SUMMER? WE DIDN'T DO ANYTHING!

SNIFF... I DON'T KNOW.

CLANG

CLANG

DON TOOK OVER, LAYING OUT THE DUTIES WE'D HAVE TO FULFILL IF WE DIDN'T WANT HER TO DIE.

THAT MEANS CLEANING THE HOUSE. TAKING OUT THE GARBAGE. MAKING DINNER AND DOING THE DISHES. TAKING CARE OF YOUR BABY SISTER. WALKING THE DOG. IF NOT... YOUR MOM WILL DIE. UNDERSTOOD?

NO SHIT.

NOW SHE WAS GOING TO LET THIS *THING* TAKE HER FROM US. *BOOZE... MEN...* SHE CHOSE THEM OVER US AGAIN AND AGAIN.

GAAHH!

THIS WAS THE *BIGGEST* BETRAYAL YET. THE *FINAL* BETRAYAL. EVERY SPLIT SECOND MY HEART WOULD ACHE AND I'D *KILL* IT WITH A ROTTEN MEMORY. HER TURNING AWAY. HER CRYING. HER *LATE* TO EVERYTHING. HER *DRUNK.*

BECAUSE I DIDN'T MATTER.

AND NOW SHE WAS GOING TO DIE ON US.

I SUMMONED ANGRY MEMORIES—LISTENING *SILENTLY* TO THE *AWFUL SECRETS* SHE'D SPILL WHILE DRINKING *ALONE* AT THE TABLE. THINGS NO SON SHOULD EVER HEAR.

NEXT UP ON DRIVE-IN THEATER...

THINK YOUR FATHER IS A GOOD MAN? DID YOU KNOW HE THOUGHT YOU WEREN'T HIS? LEMME TELL YOU SON...

WHEN I STOOD BETWEEN HER AND A DRUNKEN LOVER'S *KNIFE.* I CONJURED EVERY DARK AND MISERABLE MEMORY I HAD. EVERY ONE.

WELL...

I HARDENED MY HEART TO IT *ALL.*

...GUESS I'D BETTER START MY *CHORES.*

THE GREATEST RELIEF WAS HANGING OUT WITH *DEAN* AND *STEVE*. ONCE AGAIN I COULD *BREATHE*. WE'D RENT WHATEVER HORROR FILMS WE HADN'T SEEN AND BURN THE NIGHT AWAY, LAUGHING AND JOKING.

NONE OF US WERE *RICH, COOL,* OR HAD *GIRLFRIENDS* SO WE'D LAUGH ABOUT BEING *BROKE, UNCOOL,* AND *LONELY* AND IT MADE ALL THAT *BEARABLE.*

I'D KNOWN THOSE TWO SINCE *LITTLE LEAGUE* AND MY *UPS* AND *DOWNS* DIDN'T *PHASE* THEM. THEY LAUGHED OFF MY ROLLERCOASTER MOODS WITH *LESS* THAN A GRAIN OF SALT AND UNDERSTOOD MY *FAMILY* ISSUES.

WE HAD A "*TOUGH LUCK,*" GALLOWS HUMOR THAT DEFLATED WHATEVER *MISERY* WE WERE FACING. WE PLAYED *HOCKEY* AND WATCHED *MOVIES* AND LOST AT *POOL* AND LISTENED TO EACH OTHER'S PROBLEMS.

I DON'T THINK I WOULD HAVE MADE IT WITHOUT THEM.

BBRUUMM BUBRRAM

AWW, COME ON, THAT'S RIDICULOUS!

NAW, DUDE, THIS IS THE BEST PART! FUCKIN' CHAINSAW!

"WORKSHED"

I GOT A JOB AT A VIDEOGAME/PIZZA JOINT THAT HAD AN *ANIMATRONIC BAND*. OFTEN I HAD TO DRESS AS A *RAT*, BUT I DID IT *HAPPILY* — AS I FELL IN LOVE WITH ANY GIRL WHO WAS *KIND* TO ME.

DEAN WORKED THERE AS WELL AND WHEN OUR PAL *MIKE* WAS WORKING THE KITCHEN WAS A *CARNIVAL* OF *STUPIDITY* AND *HILARITY*.

UH, THANKS AGAIN, JIM.

ANYTIME, MELISSA!

GODDAMNIT THEY STIFFED ME!!!

—THE FUCK'S GOIN' ON OUT HERE?

OH HEY, TOM.

JESUS, YOU GUYS!

POP AND I STILL HAD OUR *ISSUES* AND IT FELT AS THOUGH GETTING SOBER MADE HIM *ANGRIER*. OUR TEMPERS WERE BOTH FIERCE AND IN *CONFLICT*.

OUR FIGHTS WERE GETTING MEANER AND MORE *SURREAL*.

WHAT THE HELL'RE YOU *DOING*, MAKING *DESIGNS*? JUST RAKE THE LEAVES! YOU AN *IDIOT*?

YEAH, I'M AN IDIOT!

WHATTA YOU CARE HOW I RAKE ANYWAY?

SMART ASS!

WHAT'S WRONG WITH YOU PEOPLE?! I'LL RAKE MY OWN LEAVES, GET OUT!!

HUFF HUFF

MAN, YOU'RE REALLY A *JERK*. CAN'T EVEN RAKE THE NEIGHBOR'S *LAWN* WITHOUT MAKIN' A *SCENE*.

OF COURSE IT'S MY FAULT. MAYBE YOU SHOULDN'T HAVE HAD ME IF YOU'D JUST END UP HATING ME, YOU KNOW.

BACK TO THAT. I DON'T HATE YOU, JIMMY, YOU'RE JUST SCREWED UP, MAN!

I DIDN'T RUIN YOUR CAREER AND IT'S NOT MY FAULT YOU GOTTA BE SOBER!

MAN, WHAT A ROTTEN KID!

WE HAD A BIG *ART* SHOW AT SCHOOL AND POP ACTUALLY SHOWED UP FOR IT. HE WAS TAKEN ASIDE BY MY ART TEACHER "ON THE Q.T."

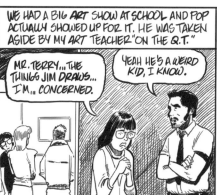

MR. TERRY... THE THINGS JIM *DRAWS*... I'M... CONCERNED.

YEAH HE'S A WEIRD KID, I KNOW.

I GOT AN EARFUL *LATER* BUT IT WASN'T *NEW*.

MAN I HAD TO LISTEN TO THAT *CREEPY CHICK* ASK IF YOU'RE SOME KINDA' *SUICIDE RISK?*

JIMMY... ARE YOU THAT *MESSED UP?*

NO I'M *NOT*, OKAY? *JEEZ* I CAN'T BELIEVE HER - IT WAS JUST A DRAWING OF THE GRIM REAPER!

WHEN POP TALKED TO *MOM* ABOUT IT SHE HAD AN ENTIRELY DIFFERENT *REACTION*.

WAIT, WHAT?

WHAT'S THIS ASSHOLE'S NAME? YES I'M GONNA CALL HER, BILL!

DID YOU BOTHER *TALKING* TO MY SON OR DID YOU SIMPLY JUMP TO A *POORLY INFORMED CONCLUSION?* HE HAS A *HEALTHY IMAGINATION* AND LIKES "SCARY THINGS", SO WHAT? TALK TO *HIM* AND HE'LL GO ON *ALL DAY* ABOUT WHO HIS "INFLUENCES" ARE I COULD TELL RIGHT NOW YOU'VE NEVER READ "CONAN", "TALES FROM THE *CRYPT*" OR "EERIE" ___ ZINE- YES I HAVE ___ SU___ ___ON AND OF COL___ ___ ___ READ IT, WHY ___ ___ ___ I? FRANKLY I'M ___ A ___ LITTLE DISTU___ THAT YOU DID___ TALK TO HIM___

I KNOW THAT *MENTAL WELL BEING* IS AN IMPORTANT ISSUE AND THAT MY TEACHER'S INTENTIONS WERE *GOOD*... BUT I WASN'T *SUICIDAL. I WAS* LONELY. I *KNEW* I WAS A WEIRDO. I *KNEW* THAT I WAS STRANGE.

WHAT KIND OF DUMBASS ART TEACHER DOESN'T KNOW WHO FRANK FRAZETTA IS?

WHAT MY MOM *DID* THAT DAY WAS TO TELL ME THAT IT WAS *OKAY* TO BE THOSE THINGS.

THANKS, MOM.

LOVE YOU, SON.

FRIDAY NIGHTS WERE FOR *MOVIES*. PAY FOR THE FIRST-SNEAK INTO AS MANY MORE AS POSSIBLE. ONE CLASSIC NIGHT WE HIT "NIGHTBREED," "THE GUARDIAN"(FRIEDKIN), AND "BLOOD OF HEROES".

THEN THE OLD LADY COMES OUT AND ME AND MY DAD ARE SLUGGIN' IT OUT.

AT LEAST YOU WEREN'T TIED TO A TREE IN YER *UNDERWEAR* BY YOUR BRO AND HIS PALS.

TRUE. HEY I READ THAT *CRONENBERG* IS IN THIS.

NICE.

DEAN AND STEVE UNLOCKED SOME CODE AND FIGURED OUT HOW TO TALK TO GIRLS. I STILL HAD NO CLUE.

I JUST DON'T KNOW IF I SHOULD *TRUST* HIM.

NO! TRUST ME, YOU SHOULDN'T!

BUT WHO ELSE IS THERE?

ME!

YOU'RE SO FUNNY.

IT NEVER OCCURRED TO ME THAT I WAS LOOKING FOR LOVE IN ALL THE WRONG PLACES UNTIL I MET D.

WHO....*IS* SHE?

BESIDES AN ANGEL, OBVIOUSLY.

SHE LAUGHED AT MY BAD JOKES AND IT WAS LOUD AND UNSELFCONSCIOUS. SHE HAD A BOYFRIEND IN COLLEGE WHO I FIGURED WAS PROBABLY *EVIL*.

HAHA!

I HATE YOUR BOYFRIEND!

I WAS UNDETERRED, HOWEVER, AND BEFORE LONG I WAS EXPRESSING MY TEENAGED LOVE IN EPIC *LETTERS, POEMS, AND DRAWINGS.*

SHE REMAINED FAITHFUL TO HER BOYFRIEND, BUT WAS ALWAYS *KIND* AND *GENTLE* IN HER REBUKES.

I MADE HER ENDLESS *MIX* TAPES AND SHE ACTUALLY LISTENED TO THEM. WE BONDED OVER BOOKS AND SHE READ THE AWFUL HORROR NOVEL I WAS TRYING TO WRITE.

I LIKE THE CHARACTER CHARLIE, BUT HE HAS SOME *ISSUES.*

OH, YEAH?

YEAH, ODDLY ENOUGH, HE REMINDS ME OF YOU.

BUT YOU LIKE HIM?

LOVE.

SHE SAID SHE **LOVED** ME. SHE ACTUALLY EXHALED AND WHILE DOING SO MOVED HER LIPS AND TONGUE SO THEY WOULD FORM THOSE *IMPOSSIBLE, MAGIC* WORDS.

I HAD BEEN SO IN LOVE WITH EVERYTHING ABOUT HER FOR SO LONG IT *COULDN'T* HAVE BEEN REAL. SHE WAS *SMART. FUNNY.* BEAUTIFUL. SHE WAS A *GOOD* PERSON.

AND SHE **LOVED** ME.

AND SHE **CHOSE** TO LOVE ME. **ME!** WHO FELT **UNLOVABLE.** SHE SHATTERED EVERYTHING I'D GROWN TO BELIEVE ABOUT MYSELF... THAT I WAS **UNWANTED.**

ALONE. OUTSIDE FOREVER.

SHE CHOSE ME.

I GAVE MY HEART TO HER COMPLETELY AND *GLADLY.*

SHE TOOK *GOOD CARE* OF IT. PATIENT WITH MY JEALOUSY AND *INSECURITY.* SHE LISTENED WITH **KINDNESS** AND **COMPASSION** WHEN I TALKED ABOUT MY *FAMILY* AND THE *HURT* I FELT.

WE LAUGHED. MY HEART SOARED.

SHE INVITED ME INTO *HER* LIFE AND I DID WHAT I COULD TO HELP THERE.

WE WENT TO **PROM.**

SHE VISITED ME AT MY JOB.

WE TALKED ABOUT *BOOKS* AND *ART.*

SHE WAS MY *GIRLFRIEND.*

SHE WAS A CHRISTIAN.

SHE HAD BOUNDARIES.

SHE HAD A CONCERN OVER MY EVERLASTING SOUL.

IT WAS BECOMING AN *ISSUE.*

I WENT TO *CHURCH* WITH HER AND HER FAMILY.

HEY THERE, GOD. IT'S JIM. THANKS FOR ALL THE GREAT THINGS IN MY LIFE. FEEL LIKE I'VE GOT A LOT TO BE *THANKFUL* FOR.

I WON'T GET INTO THE THINGS I'M *MAD* ABOUT SINCE I DON'T THINK YOU WANT TO HEAR THAT STUFF BUT YOU KNOW I'M PRETTY ANGRY. I JUST DON'T *GET* A LOT OF THINGS. THIS WHOLE *CHRISTIANITY* THING, FOR EXAMPLE.

I'M TO BELIEVE THAT ALL OF MY NATIVE ANCESTORS ARE ETERNALLY *FUCKED* JUST BECAUSE THEY NEVER HEARD OF *JESUS?* HOW IS THAT *LOVE?* I ASKED SOMEONE ABOUT IT AND THEY SAID EVERYONE IS TOLD THE *TRUTH* WHEN THEY DIE AND GET TO *CHOOSE... REALLY?*

IT'S LIKE THEY WERE MAKING IT UP, MAN! THEN HE TELLS ME THAT'S WHY *MISSIONARY* WORK IS SO IMPORTANT BUT HOW CAN HE JUSTIFY WHAT THE *JESUITS* DID? GIVING NATIVES *SMALL POX* SO THEY COULD CONVERT THEM AS THEY LAY *HELPLESS* ON THEIR *DEATH BEDS??*

WHAT ABOUT ALL THE NATIVE *KIDS* TAKEN FROM THEIR HOMES AND FORCED TO BE CHRISTIANS? WHY DOES THIS MESSAGE HAVE TO BE COUPLED WITH *INTOLERANCE* AND *ARROGANCE?* I'VE READ JESUS'S WORDS AND HE *WASN'T* ABOUT THAT! CAN YOU HELP ME OUT THERE, GOD?

ANYWAY, JUST SOME STUFF I'VE BEEN STRUGGLING WITH. THANKS FOR LISTENING AND THANKS FOR MY LIFE. I DON'T EXPECT AN ANSWER BUT ONE WOULD SURE BE NICE. AMEN.

POP RESENTED MY RELATIONSHIP WITH HER AND HER *FAMILY* FOR SOME REASON AND ONE SUNDAY I RETURNED HOME TO FIND HE'D DESTROYED MY *ROOM*, THE BOOKS AND PICTURES SHE'D GIVEN ME *TORN TO SHREDS*. I WAS *STUNNED*.

WHA... I DON'T UNDERSTAND!

WHY DID YOU DO THIS!?

ARE YOU AN *INSANE* PERSON?

I'M... SORRY, JIMMY.

YOU CAN'T... YOU CAN'T *TRUST* PEOPLE LIKE THAT.

WHAT?

WHU... WHAT A *FUCKED UP* THING TO DO! IS IT JUST BECAUSE I'M *HAPPY?* YOU CAN'T LET ME HAVE THAT? *WHY?!?*

SON—

HOW MISERABLE *ARE* YOU? I WISH YOU STILL *DRANK*. AT LEAST THEN YOU WERE *OCCASIONALLY HAPPY!*

I ONCE HEARD SOMEONE SAY THAT YOUR PARENTS KNEW HOW TO PUSH YOUR BUTTONS BECAUSE THEY *INSTALLED* THEM. WELL, I DID NOT INSTALL MY FATHER'S... BUT I KNEW WHERE SOME WERE AND I PUSHED THEM *MERCILESSLY*.

I ALWAYS DID.

YOU'RE A *PSYCHO!* I CAN'T WAIT TO BE GONE SO YOU CAN BE *RID OF ME!*

YOU WEREN'T EVEN SURE I WAS YOURS! WHAT A RELIEF THAT'D BE FOR US BOTH, HUH?!

I...

JUST GO! I'LL BE GONE SOON!

AMAZINGLY, THROUGHOUT THIS STRANGE, ROUGH AND SOMETIMES **VIOLENT** TIME HE NEVER TOOK A DRINK. I NEVER NOTICED HIS *STRUGGLE.*

IT TOOK ME MANY YEARS TO REALIZE WHAT AN ABSOLUTE *TRIUMPH* THAT WAS.

IT WAS HEROIC.

I...

THAT SUMMER WAS THE BRIGHTEST TIME OF MY *LIFE* UP TO THAT POINT. THINGS AT HOME WERE *TENSE* SO I WAS JUST *NEVER* HOME.

I THINK STEVE LIKES YOUR FRIEND.

THAT YOU, COUNCELOR?

HEY. OVERPRICED CANDY?

DEE WAS A SOURCE OF *LIGHT* AND STRENGTH. HER KINDNESS MADE EVERYTHING BEARABLE.

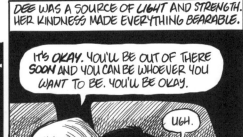

IT'S *OKAY*. YOU'LL BE OUT OF THERE SOON AND YOU CAN BE WHOEVER YOU WANT TO BE. YOU'LL BE OKAY.

UGH.

COLLEGE *LOOMED* AND EVERYTHING WOULD *CHANGE*. IT WAS HARD TO *FATHOM* AND THINGS SUDDENLY FELT MORE *PRECIOUS*, THE SMALL *MOMENTS*.

GUESS WHAT I GOT AT THE *FANGORIA* CONVENTION?

OH NO. I DON'T KNOW.

"HENRY PORTRAIT OF A SERIAL KILLER."

OKAY LET'S WATCH IT.

OH NO.

EVIL DEAD 2

CHIPS

I KNEW I WAS LEAVING ELENA WITH A HANDFUL— THE CONFLICTS I HAD WITH *POP* WERE A MIRROR OF THE ONES SHE AND *MOM* EXPERIENCED.

MOM, YOU HAVE *LUPUS* BUT YOU JUST SMOKE AND DRINK DIET *COLA*!! I MADE *DINNER*!

JEEZ 'LENA...GET OFF MY BACK, OKAY?

BUT I COULD ALMOST *TASTE* THE FREEDOM.

BOY, YOU CAN'T *WAIT* TO LEAVE.

NOPE.

JUST...DON'T FORGET ABOUT ME, OKAY?

!

BE CAREFUL. YOU'RE ALL I'VE GOT.

I WILL. LOVE YOU, 'LENA.

99

POP CONVINCED ME I NEEDED A *WELL-ROUNDED* (AND LESS EXPENSIVE) EDUCATION AND I ENDED UP IN *WESTERN ILLINOIS* - A SCHOOL KNOWN FOR *AGRICULTURE* AND *LAW ENFORCEMENT*.

JEEZ. GUESS I'M IN COLLEGE NOW...

...I DON'T THINK I FIT IN!

I WAS *CLUELESS* ABOUT *EVERYTHING* AND MY *SOCIAL LIFE* WAS *SLIM*, CONSISTING PRIMARILY OF WALKING TO THE SQUARE OR WAITING FOR MY *GIRL* TO CALL.

THAT CAN'T MEAN THAT *RUSH* IS PLAYING HERE...RIGHT?

RUSH WEEK
DELTA SIGMA

RUSH PHI BETA

EVERYONE ON MY FLOOR WAS GOING BONKERS WITH *PARTYING* BUT I COULD RESIST. IT DIDN'T MATTER HOW LONELY IT WAS BECAUSE I HAD *HER*.

HEY "ROOMIE", WE'RE GONNA HIT SOME KEGGERS. YOU IN?

THANKS, MAN. SHE'S GONNA CALL AT NINE. BESIDES, I DON'T DRINK, REMEMBER?

OK.

SHE'D GONE TO A CHRISTIAN COLLEGE AND WAS MAKING VERY CHRISTIAN FRIENDS. OUR WORLDS AND OUR VIEWPOINTS WERE BEGINNING TO DRIFT.

THEY...BURNED EVERYTHING? THEIR MUSIC? BECAUSE IT WAS SECULAR?

I DUNNO... HITLER BURNED STUFF.

WHO IS THIS LUKE GUY, ANYWAY? YOU SURE HE'S JUST A FRIEND?

I WAS WORRIED. SHE VISITED AND FELT *DISTANT*.

DID YOU...BURN THE MIX TAPES I GAVE YOU?

NO...I DIDN'T BURN ANYTHING.

WHAT'S WRONG?

...NOTHING.

SHE BROKE UP WITH ME A SHORT TIME LATER. SHE WAS REMOVING THE *SECULAR* FROM HER LIFE.

I DIDN'T TAKE IT WELL.

I DIDN'T BLAME HER... I DIDN'T THINK I DESERVED HER ANYWAY. BUT IN THAT MOMENT EVERYTHING JUST...

ALL MY FEARS WERE *CONFIRMED*. I WAS UNLOVABLE. I DID NOT BELONG TO *THIS* WORLD OR *ANY OTHER*. I WAS *ALONE*.

JUST DO IT, ASSHOLES.

I WAS NOT *WHITE* AND I WAS DID NOT FEEL *INDIAN*. I WAS A *ROGUE*, A *LONER*... NO PEOPLE, NO LOVE. I'D ACCEPT THIS FATE.

IT'S FINE... JUST LOWER ME INTO THE INDIFFERENT EARTH.

I DIDN'T *NEED* ANYONE AND NOBODY WOULD MISS ME. I'D BE A *GHOST*.

GUESS I BELONG TO THE *WASTELAND* NOW.

THERE WOULD BE GREAT *FREEDOM* IN THIS NEW OUTLOOK. COMPLETE AND UTTER *APATHY*.

WE NEED YOUR HELP, *JIM*!

I MEAN... SNAKE.

FUCK YOUR PRESIDENT AND YOUR WAR.

THE PROBLEM WAS I COULDN'T BE A RUGGED LONER - MY HEART WASN'T REALLY IN IT.

GONNA GET *FOOD*. WANNA COME WITH, "ROOMIE"?

I'M GOOD, MAN, THANKS.

OK!

IT WAS JUST BROKEN.

SLAM

...IS HE GONE?

BWAAHHH! BOOO HOO HOO HOO HOO!

I MOPED AROUND FOR A GOOD WHILE WHEN THE REALIZATION SANK IN THAT I WAS *ALONE* AND DIDN'T KNOW HOW TO *TALK* TO PEOPLE.

I WILL BE ALONE FOR THE REST OF MY LIFE.

ARE YOU WITH US, MISTER TERRY?

ALONE.

THE WEEKEND ROLLED AROUND AND IT WAS TIME TO MAKE A DECISION. I IGNORED THE SCREAMING ALARMS IN MY HEAD AND DOVE IN THE *DEEP END.*

ALL RIGHT, JIM'S COMING ALONG!

LET'S GET "FUCKED UP," ROOMIE!

YEAH, LET'S ...DO THAT.

MEET SOME GIRLS!

PAR-TAY

I THOUGHT OF MY DAD'S WARNING TO ME JUST BEFORE I LEFT.

BE CAREFUL OUT THERE, INDIO. LOT OF GUYS GET INTO HARD DRINKIN' IN COLLEGE.

I'LL BE OKAY, POP. GOT NO NEED TO DRINK.

JUST...BE CAREFUL, JIMMY. PROMISE ME, OKAY?

YEAH SURE, POP. I PROMISE. BUT DON'T WORRY, I KNOW BETTER.

...OKAY, SON.

I DIDN'T HAVE TO DRINK! I COULD JUST HANG OUT! NOBODY WAS FORCING ME TO DRINK!

TWO BUCKS. KEG'S OVER THERE.

I DIDN'T *HAVE* TO FALL INTO THAT *TRAP.* I COULD OUTSMART THE SON OF A BITCH.

HERE, JIM— TWO MORE!

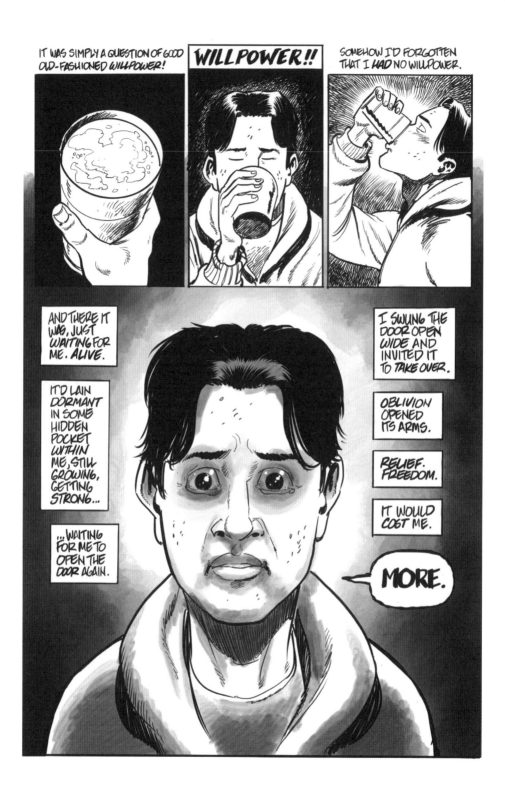

IT WAS SIMPLY A QUESTION OF GOOD OLD-FASHIONED *WILLPOWER!*

WILLPOWER!!

SOMEHOW I'D FORGOTTEN THAT I *HAD* NO WILLPOWER.

AND THERE IT WAS, JUST *WAITING* FOR ME. *ALIVE.*

IT'D LAIN *DORMANT* IN SOME *HIDDEN POCKET* WITHIN ME, STILL *GROWING,* GETTING *STRONG...*

...WAITING FOR ME TO OPEN THE *DOOR* AGAIN.

I SWUNG THE *DOOR OPEN WIDE* AND INVITED IT TO *TAKE OVER.*

OBLIVION OPENED ITS ARMS.

RELIEF. FREEDOM.

IT WOULD *COST* ME.

MORE.

NOT ALL MYSTERIES WERE AWFUL, SOMETIMES WONDER GRACED THOSE DRUNKEN NIGHTS.

DAN, WHERE THE (HIC)HELL ARE WE GOIN'?

DON'T WORRY BUDDY, IT'S COOL.

BRUM

I TRUSTED DAN SO WHEN HE SUGGESTED WE JUMP IN A CAR WITH *STRANGERS* I WENT ALONG.

KEEP UP, J.T.!

WE'RE ALMOST THERE...

AWAY FROM TOWN THE STARS *BURNED* AND I MARVELLED AS I STUMBLED FORWARD.

OKAY, YOU'VE GOT TO BE QUIET NOW...

...I'M GONNA CALL HER.

SHE MADE SOME *SOUNDS*, DAN AND I SHRUGGED. THE NIGHT WAS ABSOLUTE AND I STILL HAD A *FEAR* OF THE DARKNESS.

SHH!

SOMETHING *HUFFED* AND *SNORTED* AND A MASSIVE *SHAPE* EMERGED FROM THE SHADOWS.

WHOA.

SOMEWHERE IN ALL THIS I FELL IN **LOVE** AGAIN. SHE WAS AS *ANGRY* AS ME AND TWICE AS PASSIONATE. TALENTED AND INTELLIGENT AND *FIERCE*.

OUR FIGHTS WERE *RAW*, AS WAS OUR DEVOTION.

ONCE AGAIN I OPENED MY HEART TO SOMEONE AND SHE LIT IT ON FIRE AND PUT IT BESIDE HER OWN.

WE EACH HAD OUR BURDENS AND TRIED TO CARRY THEM TOGETHER BUT THE WEIGHT OF THOSE BURDENS *CRUSHED* US.

WE FOUGHT TO KEEP IT AND KEPT IT LONGER THAN WE SHOULD HAVE.

BOTH OF US MEDICATED WITH ALCOHOL AND IT WAS *NIGHTMARE* FUEL FOR OUR LOVE. THE END WAS PROLONGED AND SOAKED IN PAIN AND WE SUFFERED.

SHE WAS THE FIRST TO SAY THAT I WAS THE *WORST* THING TO HAPPEN TO HER.

I HOPE SHE'S OKAY OUT THERE.

THINGS WERE *TENSE* WHEN I'D RETURN HOME. POP WAS STILL *SOBER* BUT HE WAS *REELING* FROM THE DEATHS OF GRANDMA AND GRANDPA.

I WENT TO *CHECK* ON HER, JIMMY. SHE WAS JUST SITTING THERE LIKE *ALWAYS...* ...THERE WAS HALF A GRILLED *CHEESE* ON HER PLATE, MAN.

...

I THINK OF THAT GRILLED CHEESE OFTEN. GRANDPA'D PASSED EARLIER THAT YEAR... SHE MADE HER LUNCH AND SAT IN THE EMPTY HOME ALONE. SHE ATE *HALF.*

IF I *LET* THEM, THOSE THOUGHTS COULD *DESTROY* ME SO I SHUT THEM DOWN. THEY WERE *GONE* AND THAT'S ALL THERE WAS TO IT.

I'D NEVER HEAR GRANDPA *WHISTLE* OR WALK INTO A *WARM HOUSE* TO THE REASSURING SMELL OF GRANDMA COOKING SPAGHETTI FOR DINNER.

NO MORE BUTTER PECAN *ICE* CREAM OR TUCKING IN. NO MORE STRUCTURE. THE *LOVE* THEY GAVE US WAS SPINNING USELESSLY IN THE AIR, DIRECTIONLESS AND CONFUSED. THEY WERE *GONE.*

GOODBYE, GRANDMA.

I LOVE YOU.

I WAS PAINTING HOUSES AND BEHAVING BUT SOON THE URGE TO *DRINK* BECAME TOO *STRONG.*

THIS *SUCKS.* WANT TO GRAB A BEER?

LIKE YOU WOULDN'T BELIEVE, MAN.

TIRED OF SCRAPIN' THIS RICH ASSHOLE'S HOUSE!

SCRAPE SCRAPE SCRAPE

MY NEW *LIFE CHOICES* DIDN'T *GEL* WITH THE OLD MAN AND THINGS BOILED TO AN *EXPLOSION.*

GET OUTTA MY ROOM! YOU CAN'T PUSH ME AROUND ANYMORE, ASSHOLE!

THIS IS MY HOUSE AND YOU COME IN STINKING OF *BOOZE?!* YOU JERK!

GET OUT! GET OUT!

I SPENT THE REST OF MY SUBURBAN TIME IN WHAT BECAME KNOWN AS THE "HILLBILLY HILTON," A CATCH-ALL FOR THE LOCAL DERELICTS AND ROUGH EDGES, WITH STEVE'S OLDER SISTER KEEPING THINGS IN LINE... SORT OF.

YOU GUYS KEEP WATCHIN' THE SAME FUCKIN' MOVIE! C'MON-

WORKSHED

-GET OFF YOUR ASSES AND HELP ME UNLOAD THE GODDAMN BEER.

THEY WERE MY SURROGATE FAMILY AS I GREW MORE DISTANT FROM MY BLOOD. THEY DRANK, PARTIED, AND LIVED AND I WAS ONE OF THEM.

NO, IT WAS YOU! YOU SAID YOU WERE GONNA KILL ME CUZ I WAS INDIAN!

PROBABLY. HA HA HA

GLAD THAT'S FUCKIN' CLEARED UP.

WHA' HAPPENED?

MOM, MEGAN AND DON WERE IN KANSAS CITY NOW AND ELENA AND I WERE ASKED TO GET THERE ASAP. I HOPPED IN MY DELTA '88.

HEY. HOW IS HE?

IT'S NOT GOOD. HE LOOKS LIKE A SKELETON, JIM.

HM. HOW'S MOM AND MEG?

DOING THEIR BEST, I GUESS.

DON WAS DYING. HIS LIVER HAD FAILED AND HE HAD ACCEPTED THAT IT WAS HIS TIME.

JIM.

HEY, DON.

GO FOR A RIDE WITH ME?

OK.

EVERY MAN SHOULD OWN A SUIT. I'M ASSUMING YOU DON'T SO WE'RE GONNA GET YOU FITTED AND I'LL BUY IT.

YOUR MOTHER WANTS ONE LAST FAMILY PHOTO AND... YOU KNOW. I COULD CARE LESS ABOUT SENTIMENT BUT SHE WANTS IT.

YOU'LL NEED A SUIT FOR THE FUNERAL AS WELL, SO... TWO BIRDS, AS THEY SAY.

BEFORE WE WENT *IN* DON EXPLAINED TO ME THAT HE'D PUT US THROUGH THINGS NO KIDS SHOULD'VE HAD TO DEAL WITH AND THAT HE REGRETTED THAT MORE THAN ANYTHING ELSE. SAID HE WAS *AMAZED* AT THE PEOPLE WE'D BECOME IN *SPITE* OF IT AND THAT WAS GOOD.

HE WAS AN *INTELLIGENT* MAN AND MAYBE THE MOST *PRACTICAL* ONE I EVER KNEW. WE TOOK THE FAMILY PORTRAIT AND THEN HE WAS GONE.

HE'D MADE AN *AMEND* TO ME AND IT GAVE ME *PEACE*. I GOT *DRUNK* WHEN HE DIED AND WAS SICK AT HIS BURIAL, AND FOR THAT I'M *ASHAMED*.

I DID DUMB SHIT MY ENTIRE LIFE AND IT CAUGHT UP. WHAT CAN I SAY? EVEN WITH THE *LUPUS* AND ALL YOUR MOTHER WILL OUTLIVE ME.

DID HE *TALK* TO YOU?

YES.

JIM... IT CHANGED EVERYTHING.

OH DONALD, YOU SHIT. YOU *LEFT* US. I MISS YOU.

MOM AND I DRANK TOGETHER THAT NIGHT AND IT WAS WEIRD. SHE TALKED ABOUT HIM AND CRIED AS AN UNEASE SPREAD UP MY SPINE AND ALL THROUGH ME.

I WENT BACK TO SCHOOL AND TRIED TO KEEP IT OFF MY MIND BY BEING DRUNK AS OFTEN AS I COULD.

I'D TAKEN SOME OF HIS BOOKS AND HALFWAY THROUGH EUGENE IZZI'S "THE CRIMINALIST" I FOUND DON'S *BOOKMARK*. IT WAS THE LAST PAGE HE'D READ.

I MISS HIM, SON...

I'MA GET SO DRUNK I'M GONNA *SHART*.

OH YEAH? I'M GONNA GET SO DRUNK I SHART IN YOUR PANTS AND MAKE YOU *THINK* IT WAS YOU!

OH YEAH? WELL *I'M* GONNA...

DON'S DEAD.

GODDAMN GRILLED CHEESE.

OUR CREW WAS TIGHT, DRAWING AND DRINKING TOGETHER. SOMEHOW IN THE HAZE WE MADE THREE COMICS.

YOU GUYS EVER THINK ABOUT QUITTING DRINKING?

MAYBE WHEN I'M OLD...

NAH. REMEMBER OUR TEACHER QUIT FOR TWO YEARS? SAID IT WAS AWFUL.

I WAS READING TOO MUCH *BUKOWSKI* AND MY LONELINESS TURNED INTO A ROMANTICIZED SADNESS.

GO HOME, JIM! I'M NOT INTERESTED IN A DRUNK BOOTY CALL!

BOOTY CALL?!? I'M JUST TRYING TO MAKE A HUMAN CONNECTION! LET'S BE LONELY TOGETHER!

FED BY THE LEGENDS OF *DOZENS* OF TORTURED ARTISTS, I SOUGHT TO BE PART OF *THAT* LINEAGE.

ONLY THE *BEST* PEOPLE HAVE *SUFFERED!* ONLY THOSE WHO (HIC) HAVE EXPERIENCED A PROFOUND *LONELINESS* CAN CARRY A *TRUE* (BRRRP) MESSAGE!

WHO WOULD LOVE ME?? NOBODY!!

I WORKED AT A *STEAK BUFFET* AND THERE FOUND *LOCAL* FRIENDS WHO DRANK LIKE I DID.

SO DO YOUR PEOPLE WEAR FEATHERS N' SHIT? WHAT RESERVATION YOU GROW UP ON?

HEY MAN, I KNOW YOU'RE NOT *TRYING* TO PISS ME OFF BUT YOU *ARE* PISSING ME OFF!

SO SENSITIVE! JIM, WE JUST DON'T KNOW AND ARE CURIOUS!

I'M NOT.

I COULDN'T TRUST THEM WITH MY SHAME. THEY MADE ME *DIFFERENT* WITH THEIR QUESTIONS BUT I WASN'T *DIFFERENT* ENOUGH TO BE PART OF SOMETHING *ELSE.*

I DIDN'T GROW UP ON A RESERVATION.

MY DAD IS *WHITE* AND I WAS RAISED IN THE SUBURBS.

I NEVER WORE *REGALIA* AND I DON'T KNOW ANY *DANCES* OR *SONGS.* I WAS SEPERATE FROM ALL THAT.

OKAY?

SORRY, MAN. DIDN'T KNOW IT WAS AN ISSUE.

I WON'T ASK YOU ANYTHING ANYMORE...

HA HA HA

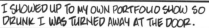

I SHOWED UP TO MY OWN PORTFOLIO SHOW SO DRUNK I WAS TURNED AWAY AT THE DOOR.

BUT IT'S MY WORK IN THERE!

I'M SURE YOU'RE VERY PROUD, BUT YOU CAN BARELY STAND.

YOU, SIR, ARE A PHILISTINE.

I GRADUATED REGARDLESS AND LEFT WITH A DECENT GPA, A COMPLETELY USELESS DEGREE, AND NO PLAN.

WELL INDIO, WE'VE HAD OUR PROBLEMS BUT I'M PROUD OF YOU. WHAT NOW?

HEH... I HAVE NO CLUE.

YOU'LL FIGURE IT OUT, SON... JEEZ, DON'T PRESSURE HIM, BILL!

YEAH, BRO?

NO, IT'S OKAY...

I WENT BACK TO PAINTING HOUSES AND WAS PROMOTED TO "FIX-UP MAN". I WAS ALONE ALL DAY.

SOME PROMOTION! FIXIN' EVERYONE ELSE'S SCREW-UPS! HUNDRED PLUS DEGREES AND I'M PAINTING SOME LAWYER'S GODDAMN MANSION!!

NOBODY TO TALK TO... JUST MY OWN POISONOUS THOUGHTS TO KEEP ME COMPANY.

I STAYED AT THE HILLBILLY HILTON THAT BLAZING HOT SUMMER AND FOUND MYSELF DRINKING ALONE WHEN NOBODY ELSE WAS UP TO IT.

THERE'S NO SOLUTION TO THIS HEAT OTHER THAN GETTING SO DRUNK YOU DON'T FEEL IT!

DAMN. FEEL SO CONNECTED TO THIS MUSIC WHEN I'VE GOT A BUZZ ON.

WE HAD PLENTY OF GOOD TIMES THAT SUMMER BUT THE SUBURBS WERE SUFFOCATING ME.

WELL, STEVE, YOU DOWN? FOUND A PLACE ON THE NORTH SIDE... READY TO HIT CHICAGO?

YEAH, FUCK IT. 'S PLACE IS DEAD ANYWAY. SIGN ME UP, BITCH.

WITH NO PLAN OR IDEA WHAT TO EXPECT I PACKED THE DELTA '88 AND HEADED TO THE CITY.

OKAY, CHICAGO, YOU SON OF A BITCH, HERE I COME.

PLEASE DON'T KILL ME.

THE SUBURBS WERE A CUL-DE-SAC AND I FELT THE NEED TO GET *LOST*. THE CITY WAS A *BEEHIVE*.

MY ORIGINAL PLAN WAS *L.A.* BUT ONCE AGAIN POP SAT ME DOWN.

"DON'T MOVE ACROSS THE COUNTRY, JIMMY... START IN *CHICAGO*. YOU CAN *ALWAYS* END UP IN L.A."

I RODE THE CTA — LEARNING, EXPLORING AND JOB HUNTING. THE ENTIRE CITY FELT LIKE OPPORTUNITY AND I WAS ELECTRIC WITH ITS ENERGY.

I WAS *FREE* AND FELT LIKE A *MAN*... BUT I ALSO BEGAN SMOKING IN HOPES IT'D CURB MY *DRINKING*.

OH YES — I COULD GET *LOST* HERE.

SO MANY ADVENTURES TO BE HAD!

MY GRANDPA TERRY CUT HIS TEETH IN THIS TOWN.

POP STARTED OUT IN THIS HERE CITY.

HE PRACTICALLY RAISED US IN IT... SORT OF.

IT WAS IN MY DNA AS MUCH AS THE WOODS OF WISCONSIN.

WE HAD AN APARTMENT ON *BELMONT* ~ I TOOK THE ATTIC ROOM, A CAVERNOUS SPACE WITH A WOODEN FLOOR PAINTED BLACK.

PERFECT.

THIS WILL BE MY DOMAIN.

STEVE WAS STILL WORKING IN THE 'BURBS AND OUR *THIRD* ROOMMATE WAS SIMPLY CALLED "THE PHANTOM" AS HE WAS NEVER AROUND... SO I WAS USUALLY ALONE.

AFTER SPENDING THE DAY TOSSING APPLICATIONS TO THE *FOUR WINDS* I'D DRINK. IF I FELT RICH IT WAS AT THE *IRISH PUB* DOWN THE STREET.

I RARELY FELT RICH SO I MOSTLY GOT WASTED AT HOME, ZONING OUT AND LISTENING TO TUNES.

HOW DO YOU THINK IT FEELS

LOU REED UNDERSTANDS.

ONCE OR TWICE A WEEK *DAN* WOULD PICK ME UP AND WE'D EXPLORE THE BARS. A *FLASK OF GIN* WOULD DIE ON THE WAY AND THEN ADVENTURE. HE HAD A *GOOD JOB* AND PICKED UP MANY ROUNDS.

HERE, IT'S GOOD FOR YOU.

I ALWAYS HAD A GOOD TIME DRINKING WITH DAN...WE GOT *ALONG* AND HE DIDN'T GET WEIRD WHEN HE DRANK - MOSTLY IT WAS ALL *LAUGHS* AND "HEAVY" CONVERSATION.

J.T....BRUCE WILLIS JUST WANTS TO BE *HUMPHREY BOGART!* THINK ABOUT IT!

DO I HAVE TO?

YES, YOU DO!

SOME NIGHTS GOT A BIT STRANGE. HUMBLING.

OKAY, DRUNKY.

HA HA!

CLOSING TIME MEANS YOU LEAVE!

AND YET... THE NIGHT IS STILL BUT A FETUS!

MOSTLY IT WAS A BIT OF A SOUR BLUR. I HAD A BITTERNESS THAT POISONED MOST THINGS.

HEY, CAN I ASK YOU SOMETHING?

SURE.

ARE YOU KOREAN?

NO... BUT THAT'S A NEW ONE.

I WAS CONSTANTLY MISTAKEN FOR ANY RACE WITH DARK HAIR. I DIDN'T TAKE IT PERSONALLY.

WELL, WHAT ARE YOU, THEN?

AMERICAN INDIAN.

YUP.

OH MY GOD, REALLY?

I'VE NEVER MET ONE BEFORE!

CONGRATS, YOU JUST MET HALF OF ONE.

NOTHIN'.

JESUS.

WHAT?

HUH?

I LOVE "DANCES WITH WOLVES."

YOU DON'T LOVE "DANCES WITH WOLVES?" BUT... WHY?

I'M GONNA ASSUME YOU'RE KOREAN. WOULD YOU LOVE IT IF EVERY KOREAN FLICK WAS 'BOUT A WHITE GUY "SAVING" YOUR FUCKIN' PEOPLE? I DOUBT IT!

STICK "DANCES WITH WOLVES" UP YER ASS.

WHAT A CREEP. **FUCK OFF!**

AND FOR YOUR INFORMATION THAT'S WHAT EVERY KOREAN WAR MOVIE IS!

GODDAMN WEIRDO.

HUH. SHE'S GOT A POINT.

I SOON GOT A SEASONAL JOB AT A *FAMOUS DEPARTMENT STORE DOWNTOWN,* BRINGING THINGS TO THE SALES FLOOR FROM THE BASEMENT.

JUST SET THAT ON THE *COUNTER,* YOUNG MAN. *THANK YOU.*

SURE THING.

I WAS HUNG OVER EVERDAY BUT COULD STILL DO MY WORK SO IT WAS RARELY BROUGHT UP. MY BUD AND CO-WORKER SHELBY HAD NO PROBLEM WITH IT.

THIS IS MY *OFFICE,* THAT'S MY *BOY JIM.* HE A *ALCOHOLIC.*

HI.

IT WASN'T HIS OFFICE BUT SHELBY OWNED EVERY ROOM HE WAS IN.

LISTEN...

...WE SITTIN' ON A *GOLD* MINE. LOOK, WE THE ONLY *STRAIGHT* DUDES *WORKIN'* HERE!

...SO?

SO? SO THESE WOMEN OUT THERE WANNA *RIDE* THE *WINNEBAGO!*

OH LORD.

I DECIDED I'D PUT SHELBY'S *THEORY* TO THE *TEST* AND ASK *JOANNA* ON A DATE, TERRIFIED.

WELL, HERE WE ARE—THE SAMPLE BOXES YOU NEEDED.

OH GOD SHE'S SO BEAUTIFUL—OK... HERE GOES!

THANK YOU! AND KID?...

YOU SMELL LIKE BOOZE

OH GOD.

EH, SHE WAS OUTTA YER LEAGUE ANYWAY, YOU IDIOT. EVEN IF SHE WEREN'T... ...YOU WOULDA RUINED IT SOMEHOW ANYWAY.

I WASN'T ENTIRELY WRONG. ALL THE WOMEN WHO SHOWED ANY INTEREST IN ME GOT TIRED OF MY ISSUES, SOME SOONER THAN *LATER*.

YOU'RE TOO *JEALOUS!* SO WHAT IF I WAS DANCING WITH HER? I TOLD YOU I LIKED WOMEN TOO...IF YOU WEREN'T SO INSECURE WE COULD'VE HAD SOME *REAL FUN!*

THAT HURTS.

I REALLY LIKE YOU BUT... YOU CAN'T KEEP CALLING ME AT *THREE* IN THE MORNING!

I'M SORRY...

YOU'RE MORE FUCKED UP THAN I AM, AND THAT'S REALLY *SAYING* SOMETHING!

GOOD CALL.

YOU SHOW UP TO MY BIRTHDAY PARTY IN A *BLACKOUT* AND GIVE ME A RAYMOND CARVER BOOK? EW.

IT REALLY WAS POOR JUDGMENT.

I'M SORRY... YOU NEED A *MOTHER* OR A *THERAPIST* AND I'M NOT EITHER OF THOSE. GOOD LUCK AND GOODBYE.

OUCH.

DON'T YOU DARE TRY AND BLAME MY DOG, SHE *KNOWS* WHERE TO PEE AND IT'S NOT IN MY BED—GET OUT OF HERE!

I'LL BE LEAVING.

NONE OF THEM WERE WRONG EITHER.

122

MANY A NIGHT WAS SPENT DRINKING WITH MY *FRIENDS*—
LOU REED, TOM WAITS, IGGY POP, LEONARD COHEN...
I SPENT *MUCH* TIME GETTING EMOTIONAL OVER THE
GUITAR SOLO IN ZAPPA'S "WATERMELON IN EASTER HAY,"
WHICH I'M SURE HE'D HAVE A CYNICAL CHUCKLE OVER.

MY *TRUE SOULMATE*, HOWEVER, WAS PETE TOWNSHEND. I
DRUNKEDLY SANG ALONG TO "EMPTY GLASS" AND
"QUADROPHENIA" LIKE THEY WERE THE *LAST ROPE*
CONNECTING ME TO LIFE.

I THOUGHT OF MY *MOM*, SINGING TO "DESPERADO."

OBVIOUSLY THE WHO WAS A FAR SUPERIOR BAND...

...SO IT WAS COMPLETELY DIFFERENT.

I SPENT MOST OF MY TIME ALONE. BOOKS, MUSIC, AND *MOVIES* WERE MY ONLY JOY BUT I DID MOST THINGS *SOLO* AND *DRINKING*.

I'M GOD'S LONELY MAN.

ANY OF YOU RYAN? PRIVATE *JAMES RYAN*?

I WAS A SHIT ROOM ATE AND STEVE MOVED OUT SO I MOVED INTO A DUMPY STUDIO IN *LOGAN SQUARE*.

BATHROOM'S DOWN THE HALL... ANYBODY WOULD USE THE SINK!

CHINASKI WOULD.

I'D RIDE THE TRAIN TO WORK AND *MARVEL* AT ALL THE *NORMAL* PEOPLE WHO WEREN'T *SICK*... WHO WEREN'T HOLDING BACK *VOMIT*.

HOW DO YOU PEOPLE DO IT?

WHAT IS YOUR SECRET?

I WAS NOW *SELLING CLOTHES* AND I WAS NO GOOD AT IT... BUT THERE WAS A *CREW* OF US THAT HUNG OUT, HITTING *CLUBS* AND SUCH.

BOOMBOMBOOMBOMBOOMPABOOMBOM

WHAT THE HELL AM I DOING HERE?

I WAS NOT THE CLIENTELE THESE ESTABLISHMENTS GENERALLY SOUGHT.

GET OUT-

-AND *STAY OUT*, YOU STUPID *DRUNK*!

OOF!

125

THE **WORK** CREW WAS A CRAZY BUNCH. LOOKING **GOOD** FOR THE **CLUBS** WAS A PRIORITY—I DIDN'T REALLY FIT IN BUT I REALLY **LOVED** SOME OF THEM.

KEEP THAT TIE, IT'S LESS HIDEOUS THAN THAT THING YOU WORE IN.

GOD, SOME POOR TRAMP IS GONNA FALL IN LOVE WITH YOU TONIGHT.

HA HA, C'MON MAN.

CAN WE GO NOW?

THE NIGHTS WERE FILLED WITH BEAUTIFUL PEOPLE IMPRESSING EACH OTHER WITH DESIGNER CLOTHES AND DESIGNER DRUGS—I HAD NO INTEREST IN EITHER.

I WAS LONELY.

I WANTED TO DRINK.

SO I HUNG AROUND AT THE FRINGES.

BOOM BOOM BOOM BOOM BOOM

WHERE'S YOUR FLASK? I NEED A NIP YOU BASTARD.

WANNA GET A TACO!?

...

YEAH CHICO, LET'S BOUNCE.

SOMETIMES THEY'D END UP AT **MY** BARS.

THIS IS WHERE YOU COME TO **RELAX**? GOD, NO WONDER YOU'RE SO GODDAM FUCKING DEPRESSED ALL THE TIME... THAT JUKEBOX SHOULD HAVE A SUICIDE HOTLINE ON IT. FUCK.

HA HA HA

HALF THE BOYS IN HERE ARE GAY AND IN HIDING, YOU KNOW.

CHEERS.

OCCASIONALLY IT'D BE THE OTHER WAY AROUND.

DAMN IT, MAN, YOU SAID THERE'D BE STRAIGHT WOMEN HERE—THERE'S NOTHING BUT SWEATY DUDES!

IT'S A GODDAMN **GAY** BAR! STOP BEING A BITCH AND **DANCE**!

I DON'T DANCE!

HA HA HA

THEY ALL SAW ME IN BAD SHAPE. THEY DRAGGED ME OUT OF BARS, PULLED ME OFF THE FLOOR, AND GOT ME HOME. THEY RAZZED ME BUT ALWAYS PICKED UP THE PHONE.

AFTER MANY YEARS I WILL RUN INTO YOU AGAIN, CHICO. WE'LL BECOME BROTHERS AGAIN.

YOU'LL GO TO THE STAR WARS MOVIES WITH MY FAMILY.

WE GO THROUGH SOME TOUGH TIMES IN LIFE.

WE'LL STAY IN TOUCH.

BUT WE'LL ALWAYS STAY FRIENDS.

WE'LL DRIFT APART.

BUT YOU WILL MISS ME AND THINK OF ME OFTEN.

VERY OFTEN, HOWEVER, I WAS ALONE AND AT THE MERCY OF MY DRUNKEN UNPREDICTABILITY.

WHAT ARE YOU WRITING?

HUH? OH. JUST A STORY.

YOU BETTER NOT BE WRITING ABOUT ME, GODDAMNIT.

WHAT?

YOU HEARD ME, ASSHOLE.

I DON'T EVEN KNOW YOU, DOUCHEBAG. WHY THE FUCK WOULD I WRITE STORIES ABOUT BAGS WITH SHIT IN THEM ANYWAY? HA HA...

...CUZ THAT'S WHAT YOU REMIND ME OF IS A BAG OF SHIT.

OOF!

WHUD WHUD WHUD

WHUMP

GASP!

ROSIE'S

SLAM!

PARKI

127

WHERE AM I? A SHOWER. *MY* SHOWER...

...DON'T THINK ABOUT IT. ERASE IT FROM THE CHALKBOARD OF YOUR MIND.

NOTHING HAPPENED. NOTHING HAPPENED.

WHAT... HAPPENED?

YOU'RE OKAY.

JUST START OVER.

START OVER.

START OVER.

THIS IS YOUR WAKE UP CALL, YOU IDIOT.

YOU'VE BEEN *LUCKY.*

YOU'RE NOT CAREFUL YOU'LL END UP DEAD ...OR *WORSE.*

BRAINDEAD OR *CRIPPLED.* WHO WOULD TAKE CARE OF YOU? *MOM?* MOM, I'M SO... SORRY.

YOU'VE FALLEN A *LONGWAY* BUT IT'S NOT TOO LATE. YOU CAN STILL GET YOUR *SHIT* TOGETHER ... JUST NEED TO STAY STRONG, USE A LITTLE BIT OF *WILLPOWER* FOR ONCE, YA DANG *BUM.* YA *CHUMP.*

ANYTHING ELSE?

YEAH, GIMME TWO PACKS OF CAMELS.

HOW DID I END UP AT THE *LIQUOR STORE?*

I'LL... START FRESH TOMORROW.

BEER

SHAME AND LONELINESS WERE A PARASITIC **TAG TEAM**.
THE CRUSHING WEIGHT OF MY DISCONNECTION DROVE ME
TO **SEEK**, WHICH OFTEN LED TO SHAME. THE **SHAME**
TOLD ME I WAS UNWORTHY OF **LOVE** AND REINFORCED
THE **LONELINESS**... AND SO ON.

I AGREE WITH JAMES JONES AND MONTY CLIFT. I SURE
AS HELL DIDN'T LIE ABOUT BEING LONELY — TO ME IT WAS
UNATTRACTIVE AND DESPERATE AND BEGAN TO FEEL LIKE
A CONTAGIOUS **SICKNESS**... OTHERS COULD **SENSE** IT AND
STAYED AWAY FOR FEAR IT'D SPREAD TO THEM.

TO **AVOID** THIS JUDGMENT I BEGAN TO **ISOLATE**, AND THE
SHAME **SHIFTED** AND LONELINESS PUT ITS HANDS AROUND
MY THROAT.

ONLY THOSE WHO HAVE BEEN REALLY, **TRULY** LONELY KNOW
THAT FEELING, THAT THEY ARE FLOATING ON A RAFT IN
THE ENDLESS OCEAN WITH **NO HOPE** OF RESCUE. NO BIRDS,
NO BOATS, NO FISH... **ALONE**.

THE TRAGIC **IRONY** IS THAT THEY ARE NOT ALONE IN **FEELING**
THIS.

WHEN I HAD A DAY OFF I NO LONGER WENT TO THE MOVIES - I STOCKED UP AND HAD MARATHONS ALONE, GLORYING IN THE DRUNKEN EMOTIONAL CONNECTION I'D FEEL WHEN JUST DRUNK ENOUGH.

OH MY GOD...**LUKE** HE'S YOUR **FATHER**...YOU'RE FIGHTING YOUR **FATHER**... (SOB) FOR YOUR VERY **LIFE**...YOU WILL DEFEAT HIM...WITH **LOVE**.....

I WAS NOT ALONE WHEN LOST IN A FILM OR A BOOK...BUT ONCE IT WAS OVER THE VOID FLOODED BACK IN.

I'D END UP WANDERING ALONE, LOOKING FOR ANY KIND OF **CONNECTION** AND USUALLY ENDING IN **BLACKOUTS** AND **MYSTERY WOUNDS**.

PROBABLY JUST FELL. NO WORRIES, NOTHING IS BROKEN.

NOTHING IS BROKEN.

THOSE BLACKOUTS WERE MAKING ME PARANOID. I DIDN'T KNOW WHAT I WAS **CAPABLE** OF, I NO LONGER THOUGHT MYSELF A **GOOD MAN**.

OKAY...YOU'RE IN A BAR SO THAT COUNTS AS **HUMAN** INTERACTION. IT COUNTS.

JUST WORK, DRAW, AND WRITE AND DON'T **TALK** TO ANYONE AT ALL.

YOU'RE NOT **LIKE** THEM.

THEN GO **HOME**.

STAY OUT OF TROUBLE.

ONCE I STARTED DRINKING I LOST ALL CONTROL SO I JUST **DRANK ALONE**. MY WORLD GOT **VERY SMALL VERY QUICKLY**.

I DIDN'T KNOW WHAT WAS WRONG WITH ME

ONE BEAUTIFUL DAY, SICK AND IN DESPAIR
I JUST JUMPED INTO THE LAKE

MY BOILING BRAIN AND GREASY SKIN
BEGGED FOR RELIEF

"TAKE CARE OF ME" I SAID, DIVING IN

I SANK DEEPER.

OCCASIONALLY I STILL MADE IT TO THE THEATER, THOUGH USUALLY WITH A FLASK. ONE NIGHT I TOOK THE BUS TO AN ART HOUSE TO SEE A FILM I WAS *CURIOUS* ABOUT.

SMOKE SIGNALS. AND I FELT LIKE I KNEW ALL THE *CHARACTERS* - THEY LOOKED AND TALKED AND *LAUGHED* LIKE PEOPLE I KNEW. NATIVES.

VICTORRR!

STOP IT, THOMAS!

THEY WERE *HAUNTED* BY THEIR LIVES BUT *LAUGHED* THROUGH IT. THEY WERE BROKEN BY ALCOHOL, BY THEIR *PARENTS*, BY THE WORLD THEY WERE BORN INTO. WHERE THEY WERE BORN.

JOHN WAYNE'S TEETH!

HEY-YA JOHN WAYNE'S TEETH!

VICTOR'S COMPLICATED RELATIONSHIP WITH HIS FATHER HIT ME LIKE A GUT SHOT. I DIDN'T WANT IT TO END...THE FINAL LINES DEVASTATED ME.

IF WE FORGIVE OUR FATHERS ...WHAT IS LEFT?

I WAS AN INDIAN...

...AND I DIDN'T KNOW WHAT THAT *MEANT.*

I'D TAKEN MANY BOOKS FROM DON'S LIBRARY AND THEY TRAVELLED WITH ME FROM PLACE TO PLACE. I'D EYEBALLED DEE BROWN'S "BURY MY HEART AT WOUNDED KNEE" FOR YEARS AND DECIDED IT WAS TIME TO GIVE IT A GO. IT UTTERLY DESTROYED ME.

I DREADED *READING* IT BUT WENT BACK LIKE A HUNGRY *VICTIM* ASKING FOR *MORE*.

HERE WAS A PLAIN-SPOKEN CHRONICLE OF "HOW THE WEST WAS WON," A FACTUAL ACCOUNT OF THE SYSTEMATIC *ELIMINATION* OF THE INDIGENOUS PEOPLE BY *ANY* HORRIFYING MEANS POSSIBLE.

WHY DIDN'T THEY TEACH *THIS* IN SCHOOL?!

BECAUSE IT WAS *UGLY* AND *CRUEL* AND OBVIOUS. BETTER TO CONSIDER IT AN *ABSTRACT TRAGEDY* THAN TO LEARN THE *DETAILS*. WHY GET SAD?

AMIDST THE *HORROR* AND *TRAGEDY*, HOWEVER, WAS GREAT *HEROISM*, *SPIRITUALITY*, AND *SURVIVAL*.

I LOOKED AROUND AND SAW THE WORLD *ANEW*. THIS *METROPOLIS* BUILT ON *BLOOD* AND *DECEIT*. THE SHEER MAGNITUDE STAGGERED ME... I WAS A *FOOL* AND A BIGGER *FRAUD* THAN I'D EVEN *IMAGINED*.

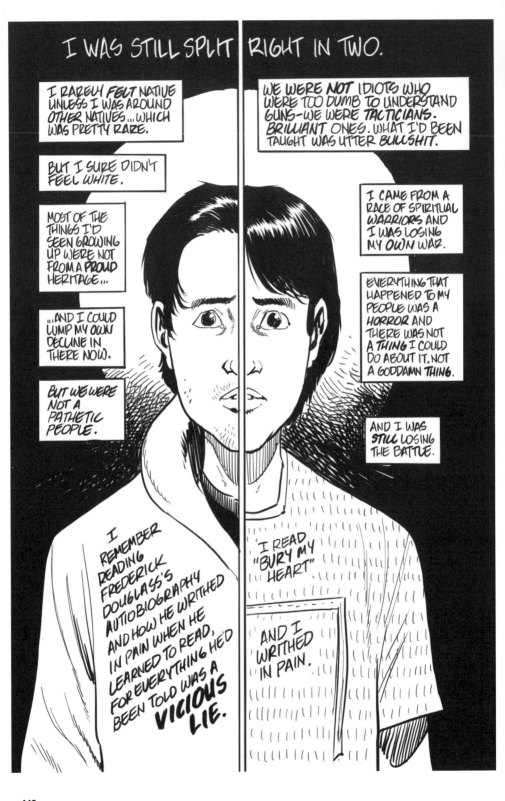

YEARS

ELENA GOT MARRIED AND HAD A BABY.
SOMEHOW I GOT MARRIED.
CHOKA AND KUNIKA WERE GONE.
GRANDMA AND GRANDPA WERE GONE.

DAD SPENT ALL HIS TIME IN PUERTO
RICO AND MOM MOVED BACK TO
THE *SUBURBS* WITH MEGAN.

MOM AND DAD WERE *SOBER*.

I CONTINUED
TO DRINK.

PASSED

I CONTINUED
TO DRINK.

I WAS NOT HUSBAND MATERIAL AND I KNEW IT. I WAS IN A CONSTANT AFFAIR WITH **ALCOHOL** AND IT TOOK ME TO AWFUL PLACES. I DISAPPEARED.

WE WERE BOTH TRYING OUR BEST BUT IT ONLY **CHANGED** MY DRINKING TO "BINGE" STYLE - I'D KEEP IT TOGETHER FOR A BIT, THEN GO **NUTS.**

I RUIN EVERYTHING.

JUST NEED TO BE ALONE.

IT NEVER **STOPPED.**

AFTER ONE DEBACLE TOO MANY I WOKE UP ALONE. SHE'D HAD ENOUGH AND SHE WAS **RIGHT** TO LEAVE. SADLY, I WAS RELIEVED.

CONGRATS, LOSER- YOU'RE ALONE NOW.

YOU CAN FINALLY DRINK HOW YOU **WANT** TO.

I STAYED ON A FRIEND'S COUCH AND SNUCK IN AND OUT, TRYING **UNSUCCESSFULLY** TO HIDE MY **DRINKING** FROM HIM. I'D BECOME A **LIAR.**

THANKS, TOM... FOUND A PLACE.

YOU GONNA BE OKAY?

I DUNNO.

FINALLY I WENT BACK TO **LOGAN SQUARE.**

IN THAT BASEMENT APARTMENT THE END BEGAN.

LORD,... AM I GONNA DIE IN THIS SHITTY ROOM?

HELLO?

142

THESE IMAGES WOULD PLAY THROUGH MY MIND OFTEN AS I SPIRALLED.

A NAMELESS, FACELESS MAN

TAKING A HELL OF A BEATING

FROM AN INVISIBLE FORCE.

HE COULD NOT STAND BEFORE BEING KNOCKED BACK DOWN BUT HE TOOK IT. WITHOUT A WORD, LIKE HE FELT HE DESERVED IT.

IT GAVE ME A STRANGE COMFORT AND I LOVED HIM FOR HIS SACRIFICE.

I RESIGNED MYSELF TO MY FATE - I WORKED AND I *DRANK* AND ALL ELSE FELL AWAY.

ALMOST TO MY STOP... MIGHT HAVE TO GET OFF *EARLY* AND *PUKE* ON THE PLATFORM...

ONCE I HAD MY *BOOZE* AND SMOKES I WAS *KING OF THE WORLD* AGAIN. THE FIRST DRINK WAS *TOUGH.*

I'LL BE OKAY... ⌐*HUCK*⌐

...ONCE I GET THIS *CHEAP* WINE DOWN...

⌐*HURK*⌐

THEN I'M SET FOR THE NEXT COUPLE DAYS.

THERE WAS NO GREATER FEELING THAN KNOWING I'D BE IN *OBLIVION* FOR A WHILE. EVERYTHING FELL FROM MY SHOULDERS AND I WAS SORT OF *FREE.*

THERE IT IS.

AND HERE WE ARE.

MY OLD FRIEND.

I'D DRINK, SMOKE, AND WATCH MOVIES UNTIL I PASSED OUT, WAKE UP AND CARRY THE DRUNK OVER.

LOOKS LIKE A NICE SUNNY DAY OUT THERE.

IT HURTS MY SOUL.

THE APARTMENT WAS A *CAVE,* THE RADIATOR WAS ATTACHED TO THE CEILING AND IT MADE SUDDEN, TERRIFYING *NOISES* OUT OF THE BLUE.

CLANK CLUNK

THE HELL... TRYNA WATCH "THE THIN RED LINE" HERE...

BOOM

CRACK CRACK PING AARGH FWOOM

MY FRIENDS STILL *CALLED* BUT I DIDN'T ANSWER. IT WAS JUST *EASIER* THIS WAY... I LOVED THEM BUT COULD *NEVER* EXPLAIN THE HOLLOW SHADOW THAT FILLED MY INSIDES. I THOUGHT IT'D *SCARE* THEM.

THE LOST, BUSTED WAY YOU FEEL RIGHT NOW IS THE WAY YOU WILL FEEL *FOREVER.*

THE ONLY ANSWER IS TO STAY *NUMB.*

OBLIVION.

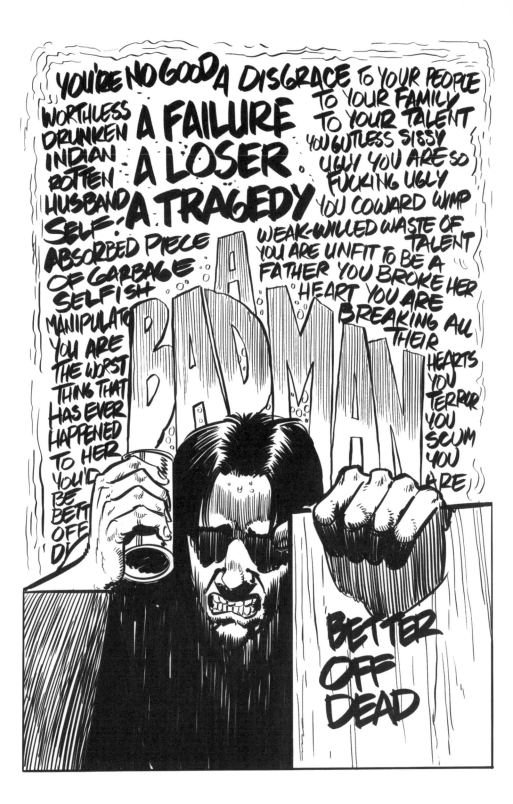

146

Sssssssssss...

KLANG

I CAN'T **KILL** MYSELF... IT WOULD DESTROY THE FAMILY... SO JUST... TAKE ME IN MY SLEEP, LORD.

DON'T LET ME WAKE UP. HAVE MERCY ON ME.

KANG CLUNK HISSSSSSSS...

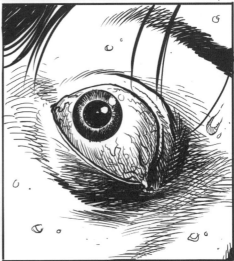

SO THIS WAS IT—MY WILLIAM HOLDEN-STYLE DEATH.

"DRUNK INDIAN DIES OF D.T.'S... ALONE. ALONE."

MY SISTER WAS RAISING A BEAUTIFUL CHILD ON HER OWN.

SHE COMMITTED TO A DEEPLY SPIRITUAL LIFE AND WAS DOING HER ABSOLUTE BEST.

MOM WAS SOBER. SURE, SHE GOT A BIT NEW-AGEY.

SURE, SHE STILL CALLED ME ON TONY'S BIRTHDAY TO TELL ME HOW OLD HE WOULD HAVE BEEN.

BUT SHE WAS SOBER.

CLAP CLAP CLAP
CLAP CLAP
CLAP CLAP

WHAT WAS I? NOT INDIAN. NOT WHITE.

JUST A DRUNK.

DAD WAS SOBER. SURE, HE SEEMED ANGRIER THAN BEFORE.

SURE, WE BARELY SPOKE AND WHEN WE DID IT WAS A GUARANTEED FIGHT.

BUT HE WAS SOBER.

I COULD NOT GO A *DAY* WITHOUT BOOZE.

I DIDN'T KNOW HOW TO *LIVE* WITHOUT IT ANYMORE.

THEY WENT TO MEETINGS, THAT MUCH I KNEW.

THERE WAS REALLY *NOTHING* TO LOSE.

SO I GAVE IT A TRY.

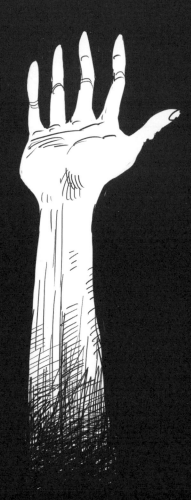

EVERYONE SEEMED TO *KNOW* EACH OTHER—AND THEY LOOKED *HAPPY* TO BE THERE. SO MANY *LAUGHING* AND *JOKING FACES*, SUCH CONTENT.

CLEARLY I DIDN'T BELONG HERE.

A YOUNG GUY CAME UP AND STARTED *TALKING* TO ME. I WAS AMAZED AT HOW *LAID BACK* HE WAS, AS THOUGH THIS WAS AN *AVERAGE DAY* AND NOT *THE END OF ALL THINGS*.

BET YOU NEVER EXPECTED TO BE IN A PLACE LIKE *THIS*, HUH? HEH.

...NO...

THIS GUY ...CHUCKLIN' AT MY *DEMISE*... WHAT GIVES?

HE WROTE HIS NUMBER IN THE BOOK I WAS READING, "PORTRAIT OF THE ARTIST AS A YOUNG MAN" AND TOOK A SEAT. I FOUND MY WAY TO THE BACK ROW AND TRIED TO *FOLLOW ALONG*.

JUST... JUST TOUGH OUT THE *HOUR*...

PEOPLE GOT UP AND TALKED ABOUT BEING SOBER... THEY WEREN'T *COMPLAINING*, THEY SHARED AS THOUGH THEY WERE ALL *MIRACLES*.

HEH HEH HA HA

I GET IT, LADY... YOU FORGOT HOW GREAT A GODDAMN MILKSHAKE TASTES. CONGRATS.

A GUY GOT UP AND TALKED FOR THE SECOND HALF. AN ELECTRIC JOLT SHOT THROUGH ME EVERY TIME I RELATED TO SOMETHING HE SAID.

I'VE FELT... EXACTLY THE SAME...

...I DIDN'T KNOW THAT ANYONE... ELSE FELT THAT WAY INSIDE...

HE WAS SO *OPEN* ABOUT TRAGIC, HUMILIATING EVENTS IN HIS LIFE AND THE JOINT WAS NODDING AND *LAUGHING ALONG*. SOON, ALTHOUGH I WAS *SHAKEY* AND *SICK*, I WAS LAUGHING TOO.

SHIT... I RECOGNIZE THIS LAUGHTER! GALLOWS HUMOR! INDIANS HAVE BEEN USING THIS FOR CENTURIES TO SURVIVE!

HA HA HA HA HA

WHEN I STARTED DRINKING I'D HAVE HANGOVERS. A *DRAG*, AN *INCONVENIENCE*. BUT AT THIS POINT— WHEN I STOPPED DRINKING I WENT THROUGH WITHDRAWAL.

IN MY EXPERIENCE THERE WAS ONLY *ONE WAY* TO KEEP THE DEADLY SYMPTOMS AT BAY AND I'D BEEN DOING IT FOR YEARS.

I HAD TO MAKE IT TO THE *FRONT DOOR*. THEN I COULD DEAL WITH THE HALLWAY AND GETTING INTO MY *APARTMENT*. ONE SHAKY, AGONIZING STEP AT A TIME.

MADE IT... GOTTA... GET THESE *CLOTHES* OFF... UGH...

YOU'RE BREAKING MY *HEART*, MI HIJO.

DAD...

SON... I DID MY BEST.

I KNOW, POP, I KNOW! HOW DID YOU GET THROUGH THIS?

CLOTHES FELT LIKE HOT SANDPAPER. ANYTHING I TOUCHED FELT HARMFUL.

OH SONNY BOY... HOW?

HOW COULD YOU DO THIS TO YOUR SELF?

I NEVER MEANT TO HURT YOU, MOM!

EVEN WATER FELT LIKE POISON IN MY GUTS.

YOU WEREN'T THERE WHEN I NEEDED YOUR *HELP*. YOU'RE MY *BROTHER*, JIM!

WHAT HAVE YOU BEEN DOING?

I'M SORRY... I'M NOT AS STRONG AS YOU THINK I AM!!!

A GRIM REALIZATION DAWNED. EVERY *STRUGGLE, TRIUMPH, FAILURE,* AND *TWIST OF FATE* FUNNELED TO THIS SHAKEY, SWEATY *WASTE OF LIFE.*

GRANDPA TERRY LIVING THROUGH *TWO WORLD WARS,* ENDLESS WARS... THE DEPRESSION... WATERGATE...LOSING THREE SONS.

KUNIKA MAKING IT OUT OF THE REEDUCATION SCHOOLS, SURVIVING THE A.I.M. YEARS... CHOKA IN COMBAT, BEING *SHOT DOWN* IN WW II...

THAT GREAT-GREAT HO-CHUNK ANCESTOR WHO EVADED THE POX, THE MILITARY, THE GOVERNMENT, AND GENOCIDE FOR *LONG ENOUGH...*

MOM RUNNING FROM HOME, DAD PLAYING MUSIC IN *L.A...* THOSE TWO SOMEHOW TAKING A CHANCE ON EACH OTHER.

ALL THE INSANE POSSIBILITIES SHOOTING, ARCING THROUGHOUT TIME AND COMING TO REST AT THIS DISAPPOINTMENT. THIS BROKEN HUSK, SWEATING OUT *BOOZE* ONTO A FILTHY MURPHY BED IN A CITY OF STRANGERS.

MY SELF-LOATHING AND GRANDIOCITY HAD REACHED EPIC LEVELS.

I TOSSED AND TURNED AND THE SHEETS WERE *FIBERGLASS* - CLINGING TO THE COLD SWEAT, PULLING AND *SCRAPING* WITH EVERY MOVE I MADE.

THIS THING....

IT'S IN YOUR *BLOOD*, MAN. ON *BOTH SIDES*. YOU'RE IN *REAL TROUBLE*, INDIO.

JUST...

MY LIMBS *ACHED*, MY STOMACH WAS AN EMPTY *CRAMP*. ANY ATTEMPT TO *PURGE* IT WAS ACIDIC *NOTHING*.

SON.... THE NIGHT WE CAME BACK FROM BURYING DON WE *DRANK* TOGETHER. IT WAS THE WORST I EVER FELT AND THE REASON I QUIT. SEEING YOU DRINK *BROKE* ME, SON.

...GOTTA....

MY BRAIN FELT LIKE A FILTHY, TOXIC COTTON BALL. INVISIBLE *MAGGOTS* WRITHED JUST BENEATH THE SKIN ON MY BACK, RIPPLES OF REVULSION.

YOU'RE BROKEN, JIM. I'M GLAD WE DIDN'T HAVE CHILDREN. YOU'RE JUST... TOO SELFISH.

...SURVIVE...

I TRIED TO ENVISION *GERONIMO* RUNNING THROUGH CANYONS, SILENT. *CRAZY HORSE* IN DEFIANCE ON THE *PLAIN*. *TECUMSEH* IN QUIET CONTEMPLATION. *CHOKA* AND HIS DAMNED *SWISHER SWEETS*. I NEEDED STRENGTH.

I GOT NOTHING.

JUST A DIRECTIONLESS *LOSS*, SWEATING OUT *BOOZE* IN THE KINGDOM OF THE *CONQUEROR*.

THERE'S A SAYING IN
THE SOBER COMMUNITY...

THAT GETTING SOBER CAN BE AKIN TO BEING—

"ROCKETED INTO THE
FOURTH DIMENSION."

IT'S USUALLY
SAID WITH A
WRY, CYNICAL
WINK.

IT'S A LITTLE
SILLY, AFTER ALL.

BUT THERE ARE
SOME WHO KNOW
THEY SHOULD, BY
ALL COUNTS, BE
DEAD.

AND WONDER...

...COULD THIS "FOURTH DIMENSION"
BE THE LIFE I LIVE EVERY DAY, AS
THOUGH IT WAS STOLEN TIME?

STEPPING INTO A *CHURCH BASEMENT* WAS BIZARRE BUT AT THAT POINT IT WAS NICE TO FEEL WELCOME ANYWHERE.

ONE FOOT IN FRONT OF THE OTHER...

OH HEY. YOU MADE IT. NICE.

HEY.

COME ON DOWN, HA HA.

AGAIN I MARVELLED AT THESE *PEOPLE.* THEY WERE ALL SO... PUT TOGETHER. LIKE THEY HAD A REASON. THEY SEEMED HAPPY.

SO... BEEN DOING A LITTLE RESEARCH?

YEAH, I GUESS.

WELL, THE GOOD NEWS IS YOU NEVER HAVE TO DRINK AGAIN.

OKAY.

HE AGREED TO *SPONSOR* ME FOR *THIRTY DAYS.* IF I COULD STAY SOBER THAT LONG WE WOULD START "WORKING THE STEPS."

I DON'T REALLY UNDERSTAND WHAT THAT ALL MEANS.

THANK YOU... FOR... YOU KNOW. AGREEING TO MEET ME.

...OKAY, SURE.

THAT'S OKAY, IT'S WHY I'M HERE.

YOU'RE HELPING ME MORE THAN I'M HELPING YOU, MAN.

WELL... YOU'VE HIT *ROCK BOTTOM.* PATHETIC LOSER. WHAT'S SO TOUGH ABOUT *DRINKING?* YOU WUSS. *WHISKEY* WOULD KILL THESE FEELINGS. *NO.* HEY THAT DUDE LOOKS LIKE A YOUNG *TOM WAITS.* WELL, IF *THAT* SUMBITCH CAN SIT THROUGH THIS MEETING YOU CAN *TOO,* ASSHOLE.

THAT WASN'T SO BAD I GUESS. THE GUY WAS ACTUALLY PRETTY FUNNY. YOU CAN DO THIS, MAN. LIKE THEY SAY, "ONE DAY AT A TIME"... JUST MAKE IT 'TIL TOMORROW.

OH GOD THIS IS **FUCKING IMPOSSIBLE!**

HE GAVE ME THINGS TO DO AND I *DID* THEM. I MADE MY *BED* IN THE MORNING AND CALLED HIM EVERY DAY. I HIT A MEETING PRETTY MUCH *DAILY*.

YEAH, I'M WALKING UP TO THE MEETING NOW. SURE ARE A HELLUVA LOT OF PEOPLE HERE.

DON'T WANT TO GO IN BUT I SAID I WOULD.

THIRTY DAYS. I STARTED "WORKING THE STEPS." WE READ FROM THE "BIG BOOK" TOGETHER.

ARE YOU EVER EMBARRASSED TO BE READING OUT LOUD WITH ANOTHER DUDE?

OH *ABSOLUTELY.* BUT THANKFULLY WE BOTH SAID WE'D GO TO ANY LENGTHS TO STAY *SOBER*, EVEN *EMBARRASSING SHIT.*

RIGHT?

RIGHT.

I'D BEEN *PASSING OUT* FOR SO LONG I DIDN'T KNOW HOW TO *FALL ASLEEP* ANYMORE, SO I READ UNTIL I DOZED OFF AND WOKE AT 6:00 AM *REGARDLESS.* AFTER A COUPLE WEEKS I FELL INTO A ROUTINE.

ANXIETY AND PARANOIA REMAINED, I HAD THE AWFUL FEELING I'D BE STABBED ON THE STREET AND I ONLY RELAXED IN THOSE *CHURCH BASEMENTS.*

SO HOW'S IT GOING?

HUH? THE HELL DO YOU MEAN?

HEH! RELAX! JUST ASKIN' HOW YOU ARE!

OH! UM... OKAY. I'M DOING OKAY.

I LEARNED MY BODY CRAVED THE SUGAR IT USED TO GET FROM *ALCOHOL*, SO—

HOLY SHIT! I FORGOT HOW GOOD MILKSHAKES ARE!

MM, YEAH, WELCOME TO SOBRIETY.

SO WORTH DESTROYING OUR LIVES SO WE COULD ENJOY SHAKES AGAIN.

HA HA HA

I IDENTIFIED AS AN ALCOHOLIC AND WAS NOT ALONE. I KNOW NOW THAT IT BROUGHT DOWN ALL RACES, CREEDS, GENDERS, AND *FINANCIAL* STATUSES EQUALLY.

IT WORKS IF YOU *WORK IT SOBER.*

I SAID ALL THE CORNY SHIT AND I *MEANT* IT.

I STARTED FEELING *BETTER*... BUT A DREAD *FEELING* GREW THAT IT WAS ALL A *DREAM* AND THAT I'D *DIED* DURING THAT LAST NIGHT.

OKAY, SPONS, LEVEL WITH ME... THIS ISN'T ALL A "JACOB'S LADDER"-STYLE DEATH DREAM?

..NO, JIM. SADLY, IT'S REAL.

I MET MY KIND OF *PEOPLE*. FUNNY AND *CYNICAL*.

BOY I'LL BE HONEST, I'M GLAD I'M AN ALCOHOLIC. YOU KNOW?

SERIOUSLY? FUCK NO. I RUINED MY GODDAM *LIFE*!

KNOW WHAT I'M SAYIN.

WISH I STAYED IN THE *MATRIX*."

THE FRIENDS I MADE WERE *COMMITTED* TO SOBRIETY BUT STAYED *HILARIOUS* AND *BIZARRE*.

I SHOULD GET MY *TEETH* FIXED.

I THOUGHT ABOUT THAT *TOO* AND THEN I THOUGHT, "WHY, SO I CAN BUILD MY CONFIDENCE UP AND GO CHEAT ON MY *WIFE*?" **FUCK THAT SHIT.**

FAIR.

GOTTA THINK IT THROUGH.

I WAS BROKE, BUT OTHERS IN THE ROOMS THREW WORK MY WAY. HOUSEPAINTING, CONSTRUCTION, WHATEVER. SOMETIMES THESE GUYS JUST *CARRIED* ME.

JUST TAKE THE FUCKIN' MONEY, JIMMY.

YOU *NEED* YOUR GODDAMN *PHONE*. PAY THE *BILL*.

...I'LL GET YOU BACK.

I KNOW THAT, MAN!

SIXTY DAYS CAME ALONG. I DUG MYSELF IN *DEEPER* WITH MEETINGS AND MY SOBER PALS. I *LAUGHED* AGAIN AND REALIZED HOW LONG IT HAD BEEN SINCE I'D *DONE* SO. A *SHOCK*.

HA HA HA HA

WITH THAT *LAUGH* I UNDERSTOOD THE *GOAL*. QUITTING DRINKING WAS JUST THE *BEGINNING*... THE *OBJECTIVE* WAS TO BE COMFORTABLE IN MY OWN SKIN.

COMFORTABLE IN MY OWN *SKIN*.

MY OWN SKIN.

I WENT TO THE MOVIES WITH **STEVE** AND CAME **CLEAN** ABOUT MY NEW SOBRIETY, WORRIED HE'D THINK **LESS** OF ME. I SHOULD'VE KNOWN BETTER.

IT'S ABOUT **FUCKIN' TIME**, ASSHOLE.

HEH.

ALL RIGHT.

SIX MONTHS ROLLED AROUND AND I WENT TO EVERY SOBER FUNCTION I **COULD**. I STILL THOUGHT ABOUT DRINKING ALL THE TIME, ITS PULL WAS **STRONG**.

DAMN IT, THAT LOOKS FUN.

BUT THAT'S A **FANTASY**, JIM. THAT'S NOT YOU AND IT NEVER WAS... YOU'D HATE IT IN THERE ANYWAYS.

I GOT A JOB AT A SMALL BOOKSTORE AND HAVING SOMEWHERE TO BE HELPED. RIDING MY BIKE EVERYWHERE, I BEGAN TO FEEL **HEALTHY, STRONG**.

IF YOU LIKE SAM FULLER YOU NEED TO SEE THE **NAKED KISS**. I'LL BRING IT IN AND YOU CAN BORROW IT.

THANKS, MIKE!

YET WAVES OF PROFOUND MELANCHOLY STILL STRUCK OUT OF NOWHERE, A **CRUSHING HOPELESSNESS**.

IT'S **NOT FUTILE**. HOW YOU FEEL RIGHT NOW IS **NOT** HOW YOU'LL FEEL FOREVER.

TOUGH IT OUT.

IT WAS EXPLAINED TO ME THAT IF I WAS TO STAY SOBER I'D HAVE TO DO THE "HIGHER POWER" THING, BUT MY MIXED PAST WITH RELIGION GAVE ME **PAUSE.**

...I DON'T KNOW HOW TO BELIEVE IN YOU, MAN.

I **GET** IT. YOU DON'T NEED TO. YOU JUST NEED TO BE WILLING TO BELIEVE IN SOME-THING **BIGGER** THAN YOU.

YOU MEAN... LIKE **NATURE?**

SURE, THAT WORKS. USE **THAT** FOR NOW.

GUESS...GUESS I COULD DO THAT.

FANTASTIC. NOW GET LOST, I GOT OTHER SHIT TO DO.

169

I WAS SOBER NOW, BUT DIRECTIONLESS.

HMM. WILL EISNER. ALWAYS HEARD OF HIM. DAMN, THIRTY BUCKS, THOUGH? GROAN...

MY GOD...THIS IS BEAUTIFUL. IS HE USING A QUILL OR A BRUSH? MAN... HE LOVES TO DRAW AND YOU CAN JUST FEEL IT...IT'S JOYFUL AND TRAGIC.

IT'S ALL A STATEMENT ON THE HUMAN CONDITION! IT'S UNLIKE ANYTHING I'VE EVER READ!

MY HEART...

...MY SOUL!

THIS GUY IS SHOWING ME THERE ARE NO LIMITS TO WHAT YOU CAN DO IN GRAPHIC STORYTELLING. THIS BOOK MOVES ME.

I NEED TO DRAW AGAIN!

A FIRE WAS LIT. I BOUGHT SOME BRUSHES AND GOT DOWN TO SOME STORYTELLING.

I'LL FINISH MY CRIME SAGA... WHAT THE HELL ELSE DO I HAVE TO LIVE FOR OTHER THAN STORYTELLING?

I SOON REALIZED ADMIRING BRUSHWORK AND SUCCESSFULLY DOING IT WERE WORLDS APART. I SUDDENLY HAD A NEMESIS.

OKAY BRUSH... THINK YOU GOT ME BEAT? I'M GONNA BREAK YOU, FOOL, I'M GONNA BREAK YOU! WORK WITH ME HERE!

MOST OF THE FRIENDS I'D MADE DISAPPEARED. IT WAS EASIER TO GET SOBER THAN TO STAY SOBER. I WAS *TERRIFIED* OF DRINKING AND STUCK TO MY PROGRAM.

YO. WHERE'S JOHN AT?

HE'S OUT DRINKIN'!

DAMN IT, I LIKED THAT GUY.

MEETINGS, *HANGING OUT*, AND *WORK* WAS MY ROUTINE AND I FOUND THE STRUCTURE *COMFORTING*. ALL MY REMAINING *FREE* TIME WAS DEVOTED TO THE BRUSH.

I'M GETTING A *LITTLE BETTER*... BUT I STILL SUCK. AND YET...

...I REALLY LOOK FORWARD TO THESE NIGHTS.

MR. EISNER, YOU PASSED ON *BEFORE* I COULD EVER MEET YOU...

...BUT YOUR *WORK* GAVE ME A REASON TO CONTINUE. I LOVE THE BRUSH, TOO. *THANK* YOU FOR YOUR WORK. THANK YOU SO MUCH.

THEN A GREAT *JOY* UNFOLDED. THE BRUSH BEGAN TO WORK *WITH* ME AND WE *DANCED*. FRUSTRATION LIFTED LIKE MORNING FOG AND A *WORLD* OPENED.

THIS FEELS...

EXACTLY RIGHT.

THE TENSION IN MY CHEST LOOSENED. I SUDDENLY FELT STRANGE. IT WAS *HAPPINESS*.

I...CAN *BREATHE!*

I FEEL LIGHT AS A *GODDAMN* FEATHER! THE HELL IS THIS?

RELIEF. SIMILAR TO THE GUSH OF RELAXATION I'D GET FROM A *DRINK*, BUT *DIFFERENT*. THIS, FELT...THIS FELT *REAL*. IT FELT EARNED.

WHATEVER THIS IS...

IT'S NICE.

"OLD GUY WHO'S BEEN SOBER FOR MANY DECADES," CAN YOU EXPLAIN THIS *TENSION* LEAVING MY GUT?

SURE, YOU UNGRATEFUL LITTLE SHIT!

MUCH OBLIGED.

OK. YOU'VE GOT THE *KNOT* IN YOUR GUT FROM ALL THE AWFUL SHIT YOU'VE SEEN, DONE, OR HAD DONE TO YOU, RIGHT?

SURE DO.

AND HOW! I ALWAYS CALLED IT THE *STEAM VALVE.*

AND THE DRINK OR DRUG...IT *RELEASES* THAT KNOT, YES?

...GOOD FOR YOU. SO BACK TO WHAT I WAS SAYING, WHAT EVENTUALLY HAPPENS WITH THAT?

THE KNOT... ISN'T ACTUALLY GONE.

WELL NO, BUT... HERE—

"THIS IS WHAT YOU *CARRY* INSIDE.

THE DRINK GIVES YOU A *FEELING* OF RELIEF—

—BUT IT'S NOT *REAL* RELIEF, THE PROBLEMS ARE STILL THERE.

SO YOU GET SOBER AND START DOING ESTEEMABLE ACTIONS—WHAT YOU THINK OF AS 'BEING A GOOD MAN'.

DON'T GET ME *WRONG,* YOU'RE STILL AN INSECURE *HOTHEAD* AND A *PERVERT,* BUT YOU STOP CAUSING THIS IMMEDIATE DAMAGE.

THE KNOT LOOSENS FOR REAL, AND IT'S NOT A BOOZY ILLUSION. IT IS *EARNED.*"

THANKS, "OLD GUY WHO'S BEEN SOBER FOR MANY DECADES," THAT'S HELPFUL.

REMEMBER—JUST BECAUSE YOU'RE NOT DRINKING DOESN'T MEAN YOU'RE NOT A PERVERTED, INSECURE HOTHEAD!

MM. HEARD THAT.

AND SO LATER—

SO HERE'S HOW I UNDERSTAND IT. DO YOU HAVE THAT *KNOT* IN YOUR GUT LIKE I DO?

YES, I DO.

GOOD. WELL THAT KNOT— WHEN YOU TAKE A DRINK—

—GOES AWAY.

172

FOR SO LONG I WAS *FUELED* AND *PROPPED UP* BY *BOOZE*. LIFE WITHOUT IT COULD BE *TERRIFYING*. EVERYTHING BECAME A TEST OF FAITH AND COURAGE.

OKAY. TODAY IS THE DAY.

THE DAY I **OPEN THE MAIL.**

THE PARANOIA FADED BUT FEARS I'D ALWAYS *DULLED* WITH *DRINK* CAME BACK IN SHARP FOCUS.

GOD, EVERYTHING IS *PHOTOREALISTIC* SUPERHEROES! THAT'S NOT YOU!

THERE'S NO ROOM FOR WHAT YOU DO!

GRAPHIC NOVELS

COMICS

THE BOOKSTORE WILL CLOSE SOON AND YOU'LL BE HOMELESS.

I HAD TO GO DEAL WITH THE *IRS*... IN MY STUPOR I'D FAILED TO *FILE* FOR A FEW YEARS AND I OWED.

OKAY *HIGHER POWER* I'M PUTTING THIS ON YOU! I'LL TAKE HOW IT GOES AND *DEAL* WITH IT.

BUT YOU'VE GOT TO TAKE AWAY THIS *CRIPPLING FEAR.*

I'M ALL IN! NOT DIPPING MY TOE IN THE WATER, I'M GOING FULL *INDIANA JONES.*

REMEMBER "THE LAST CRUSADE"? INDY HAD TO FIGURE OUT THESE PUZZLES OR HE'D *DIE*. ONE WAS AN *INVISIBLE BRIDGE* OVER A GIANT CHASM.

INDY DIDN'T MESS AROUND, HE STUCK HIS FOOT *WAY* OUT FOR THAT FIRST STEP.

THAT'S HOW I SAW *FAITH*, ALL OR NOTHING. EITHER I WAS GOING TO MAKE IT THROUGH OR I WASN'T. AND WHEN THE DAY CAME THAT I DIDN'T... THE HOPE IS THAT THE GOOD TIMES WEREN'T *WASTED* *WORRYING* ABOUT THINGS I COULDN'T *CHANGE.*

TERRY? TERRY!

OH SHIT. HERE GOES.

IT TOOK OVER *FIVE YEARS* TO SQUARE UP WITH "UNCLE SAM" AND WHILE I DON'T LOVE PAYING FOR BOMBS AND SPIES AND SHIT I TELL MYSELF ALL MY TAX MONEY GOES TO THE *NATIONAL PARKS.*

WALK THROUGH ALL THE FEAR.

TERRY? TAKE A SEAT.

NINE MONTHS CAME ALONG, I CONTINUED TO "WORK THE STEPS." IT WAS TIME TO MAKE "AMENDS" AND MY SPONSOR SUGGESTED I START BIG.

WELL, KID? WHAT'D YOU WANT TO TALK ABOUT?

I STILL FELT THE SAME RESISTANCE, THE FEAR TO OPEN MYSELF UP TO HIM. I HAD TO DO THIS BUT I WAS TOO TERRIFIED TO CONTINUE.

UM....

I WAS RULED BY FEAR... BUT IT COULD MOTIVATE.

IF I TRULY BELIEVED IN THIS HIGHER POWER I COULD TURN THIS FEAR OVER TO IT AND BE FREE. THIRTY YEARS' WORTH OF FEAR.

UH....

JIMMY.

IT'S COOL, SON. I'M YOUR OLD MAN. YOU CAN TELL ME WHAT'S GOING ON.

WHAT'S HAPPENING?

TRULY BELIEVE.

WELL SPIT IT OUT, MAN. I AIN'T GOIN' ANYWHERE.

POP...

...I'M SOBER.

...

GOOD, SON.

GOOD.

I MADE MY **AMENDS** TO HIM. I'D WRITTEN A LONG LETTER CHRONICLING THE **WRONGS** I'D DONE HIM AND JUST **READ** THE THING.
MY SPONSOR'D GONE OVER IT AND REMOVED ALL THE **PASSIVE AGGRESSION** I'D SNUCK IN THERE.

THEN IT WAS QUIET.

AFTER A WHILE HE **BROKE** THE SILENCE.

YOU KNOW, JIMMY... I WASN'T ALWAYS THE BEST FATHER, BUT I HOPE YOU KIDS KNOW I **ALWAYS** TRIED MY BEST. YOU GUYS HAD SOME TOUGH TIMES.

DAD, I **KNOW** YOU DID!

I'M **PROUD** OF YOU SON. IT'S NOT EASY KICKIN' THE BOOZE BUT YOU **DID** IT. NOW YOU CAN DO ANYTHING YOU WANT TO, MAN.

DOING THAT AMEND WASN'T EASY EITHER.

TAKES A REAL **MAN** TO DO THAT.

I NEVER DID.

WE **HUGGED** AND **LAUGHED** AND I FELT AS THOUGH I WAS A **CHILD** IN MY FATHER'S **ARMS**. I COULD SMELL THE **EARTH** IN HIS CLOTHES AND THE SHOULDER BONE AGAINST MY **CHIN** AND HE WAS JUST A MAN AND I WAS JUST HIS **SON**.

LOVE YOU, INDIO.

LOVE YOU TOO, POP.

I MADE AMENDS TO MOM.

SON I'M SO HAPPY. I WAS WORRIED ABOUT YOU.

I KNOW YOU WERE, MOM. I FELT IT.

NOW YOU CAN SPEAK AT THE MEETING I RUN IN WESTMONT.

!

OH... KAY.

I TOOK A TRAIN TO THE DELLS TO SEE ELENA.

ALL RIGHT, LET'S GET THIS DONE WITH.

WAIT-YOU READ IT?

LOOK, IT'S WEIRD FOR ME, TOO.

(SIGH) OKAY.

WE BOTH CRIED AS I READ THE AMEND— SOMEHOW EVERYTHING WE'D BEEN THROUGH RESONATED BETWEEN US AND WITH EACH SENTENCE I FELT A WEIGHT DRIFT OFF, FLOATING TO THE SURFACE, TO THE LIGHT.

SHE'D BEEN THROUGH SO MUCH WHILE I WAS WASTING AWAY. IN MANY WAYS SHE WAS ALONE AMONG OUR PEOPLE AND SHE'D WEATHERED IT ALONE.

IS THERE ANYTHING I CAN DO TO MAKE UP FOR THESE WRONGS?

JUST BE HERE FOR US ONCE IN A WHILE.

I WILL.

SOMETHING WAS RESTORED. HOW FOOLISH OF ME TO HAVE EVER THOUGHT I WAS ALONE.

LOVE YOU, 'LENA.

GOOD TO HAVE YOU BACK, YA BIG JERK.

SOMETIMES YOU JUST FORGET.

IN THE '70s POP TRAVELLED TO PUERTO RICO TO PLAY *MUSIC* AND HE FELL IN *LOVE* WITH THE ISLAND.

AFTER GRANDMA AND GRANDPA PASSED HE STARTED SPENDING ALL THE TIME HE COULD THERE.

HE SPOKE FLUENT SPANISH AND BEFORE LONG HE WAS A SEMI-RESIDENT.

WHEN I'D BEEN SOBER LONG ENOUGH THAT HE DIDN'T THINK IT WAS A *FLUKE* HE FLEW ME OUT.

"I'M UP SEEING ELENA A LOT BUT YOU AND ME, WE'VE NEVER REALLY HUNG OUT.... *LOOK,* THIS IS FOR CHRISTMAS AND YOUR BIRTHDAY, MAN, SO DON'T GET USED TO IT, COOL?"

"OKAY POP, I WON'T."

HE RENTED A CAR AND WE DROVE THROUGH THE MOUNTAINS. I'D NEVER SEEN ANYTHING *LIKE* IT.

BEAUTIFUL, HUH JIMMY?

YUP.

-SIGH- THIS KID SHEESH. "YUP"

DIG, YOU KNOW WHAT PEOPLE FROM PONCE SAY, MAN? "PONCE'S PONCE... THE REST IS PARKING." HA HA!

JEEZ. SO THEY'RE A-HOLES?

COME ON, MAN, DON'T BE JIVE. THEY *LOVE* WHERE THEY LIVE, INDIO!

HA HA

I WOULDN'T SAY WE BONDED — WE STILL ARGUED LIKE IDIOTS — BUT WE WERE BOTH *TRYING*.

C'MON, MAN! YOU SAID THERE WAS A MEETING — WELL, WHERE THE HELL IS IT?!?

I DUNNO, OK?! I'M NOT THE ONE WHO LIVES HERE! AND I DON'T SPEAK SPANISH!

I TOLD YA TA LEARN IT, MAN!

WE FOUND THE MEETING AND HE MADE IT PART OF HIS REGULAR ROUTINE. HE WAS HAPPY.

YEAH MAN, THAT WAS PRETTY FAR OUT, HITTING A MEETING WITH MY SON, MAN. EH, INDIO?

YEAH... A REAL STRESS RELIEVER.

PUNCH

PUERTO RICO WAS UNLIKE ANYWHERE I'D EVER BEEN. I'D NEVER SEEN A RAIN FOREST.

THE WORLD IS OPEN TO YOU, JIMMY. YOU DON'T HAVE TO BE "LOBO DOMESTICATO."

WHY GO BACKWARDS?

POP...

...I'M NOT EVEN SURE WHO I *AM* OR WHO WOULD *HAVE* ME, LET ALONE WHO'D HAVE ME BACK...

...I WAS QUITE A DIFFICULT PERSON.

YEAH MAN YOU'VE GOT THAT WHOLE GUILT THING GOIN'. YER GONNA DO WHAT YOU WANNA, JUST THINK IT OVER.

HERE WE ARE!

STAND OVER THERE, BY THE WATER...

OKAY.

...COOL, COOL...

MAN, JIMMY—

—YOU LOOK LIKE A REAL, INDIAN, SON!

...REALLY?

YEARS PASSED.
SOBER YEARS.

GOOD TIMES.
BAD TIMES.

LIFE HAPPENED.
I STAYED SOBER.

GURGLE
HISS POP
GURGLE

COME ON, COFFEE. I NEED YOU MORE THAN YOU COULD POSSIBLY KNOW. ANOTHER DAY. THIS IS MY LIFE. STAY GRATEFUL, ASSHOLE. YOU'RE LUCKY TO BE ALIVE, FOOL!

SOBRIETY AND MEETINGS WERE PART OF MY LIFE AND I GUARDED IT *JEALOUSLY* BUT THE ACHE FOR *OBLIVION* WAS NEVER TOO FAR AWAY.

SURE I MISS IT, THINK ABOUT IT SOMETIMES.

BUT I'D LOSE EVERY-THING THE MOMENT I DRANK. I'D GO RIGHT BACK TO THAT CAVE.

THE IDEA FOR ME IS TO BUILD A LIFE I DON'T WANT TO LOSE.

HM.

THE SAME MEETINGS, YEAR IN, YEAR OUT. GETTING SOBER DIDN'T STOP MY HEAD FROM TELLING ME I WAS *WORTHLESS* BUT NOW I HAD TOOLS TO FIGHT IT.

YOU ARE THE WORST THAT EVER HAPPENED TO HER, YOU BASTARD... —ASK JOHN HOW HE'S DOING, NOW!

AW HEY, JIM T. I'D COMPLAIN, BUT WHO WOULD LISTEN, Y'KNOW? THINGS'RE GOOD.

JOHN! HOW'S IT GOIN'?

YOU BULL-SHITTIN' ME?

I AM THINGS SUCK!

HA HA HA!

I STRUGGLED TO STAY GRATEFUL EVERY DAY BUT OFTEN *FEAR* DUG ITS TEETH IN DEEP.

OKAY... IF I CAN SELL SOME *ART* (YEAH RIGHT) AND MY *COMIC* COLLECTION I CAN KEEP THE HEAT ON BUT FUCK... THE RENT!

I'M REALLY GRATEFUL TO BE HERE!

I'M FUCKED.

OCCASIONALLY A *VOICE* WOULD INTERRUPT MY MAUDLIN REVERIES TO REMIND ME I WAS LUCKY.

HERE WE ARE AGAIN.

WAITIN' ON THE BUS TO GO SELL ART SUPPLIES. GUESS THIS IS MY "LIFE." GUESS FEELING USELESS AND A WASTE IS THE REST OF MY LIFE. OH GOD.

WAIT—HOW DO YOU *KNOW* THESE AREN'T ACTUALLY GREAT DAYS AND YOU'RE WASTING THEM *BITCHING*?

WHOA.

GO BLUE ISLAND

AT SOME POINT DURING MY DRINKING I'D THROWN SOME *SAMPLE PAGES* ON THE TABLE OF THE *CROW* CREATOR *JAMES O'BARR* AT A COMICON.

CAN YOU SIGN IT "TO LOUIE"?

I LOVE THE CROW.

HERE.

HUH?

SOME *FOUR YEARS LATER* HE SENT AN EMAIL TO SAY HE'D *LIKED* THEM AND WE BECAME *FRIENDS* OVER OLD *MOVIES, BOOKS,* AND *ARTISTS.* WE BOTH ALSO UNDERSTOOD *LONELINESS* AND THE *GREAT MELANCHOLY,* HAVING SPENT PLENTY OF TIME THERE.

HOLY SHIT! JAMES SENT ME E.C. BOOKS FROM ITALY!

AND SOME DEPRESSING MOVIES TOO!

I FLEW TO *DALLAS* AND DID SOME *SHOWS* WITH HIM. THE DRIVE TO *AUSTIN* WAS A STORYTELLING *CONFESSIONAL* AND WE LAUGHED PLENTY.

...THOSE WERE DARK TIMES FOR ME. DO YOU EVER MISS IT? DRINKING?

HELL YEAH. I MISS *OBLIVION.* BUT I WAS KIND OF A PIECE OF SHIT HA HA —

I WAS *AMAZED* AT THEIR COMICS COMMUNITY.

MAN, I DON'T THINK CHICAGO EVEN *HAS A* DRINK & DRAW!

I'D BET YOU DO, YOU JUST *ISOLATE* WITH YOUR *WORK.* IT'S THERE—

—YOU GOTTA GO FIND IT.

I FOUND IT—EVERYONE SEEMED TO *KNOW* EACH OTHER AND *HOVERED* AROUND THE *SUCCESSES.*

WHOA, IS THAT THE NEW *DC* BOOK YOU'RE WORKING ON?

YEAH.

I'LL BE DAMNED IF I'M GONNA *BUZZ* AROUND HIM LIKE A DAMNED FLY....I DON'T BELONG HERE ANYWAY!

SOON ENOUGH I ABANDONED MY SNAP JUDGMENTS AND MADE SOME DAMNED GOOD FRIENDS, DOING THE COMICON CIRCUIT AND *WORKING* ON MY *CRAFT.*

HE ASKED IF YOU WANTED TO DO A *CROW COMIC?* HOLY SHIT!

YUP.

THAT'S GREAT NEWS, JIM.

WHEN I QUIT DRINKING I WAS WORRIED ABOUT **INSPIRATION**-LOSING THAT "HIGH WHITE NOTE"~THE PERFECT **BUZZ** LEVEL THAT SEEMED TO OPEN THE **MIND** AND THE **HEART**.

I WAS **TERRIFIED** OF LOSING THAT **MAGIC**.

WHAT I DISCOVERED IN SOBRIETY WAS THAT THE **MAGIC** WAS UTTER **FANTASY**. THE INSPIRATION CAME FROM **HARD WORK** AND **DISCIPLINE**, AND I'D BEEN **EAGER** FOR STRUCTURE AND A **WORK ETHIC**.

I WORKED HARD.

I MADE MY DEADLINES AND I DIDN'T PHONE IT IN. WILL EISNER DIDN'T MISS DEADLINES - BERNIE WRIGHTSON, JACK DAVIS, JOHN SEVERIN, THEY **ALWAYS** TURNED IN TOP-NOTCH WORK.

MY **HEROES** CHANGED, MY WORK IMPROVED, MY **LIFE** CHANGED.

I WAS DRAWING **COMICS**!

POP AND I MET FOR MORNING TACOS EVERY FEW SUNDAYS TO CATCH UP. IT WAS NICE.

YEAH MAN, I WAS UP IN THE DELLS LAST WEEK, ELENA TELL YOU?

YEAH I TALKED TO HER THE OTHER DAY, YOU DID THE BIRTHDAY THING.

HER AND ZOE AND YOUR COUSINS ALWAYS TAKE ME OUT TO EAT.

AS WE TALKED, A SINKING DREAD SETTLED IN ME. I NOTICED THE LOOSE SKIN ON HIS ARMS, THE DARK, SUNKEN LOOK OF HIS EYES.

THE MEXICAN PLACE. THEY LIKE IT SO I GO ALONG WITH IT.

I THINK YOU LIKE IT TOO, HA HA.

YEAH MAN, I DO.

HOW YOU DOING?

I'M GETTIN' OLD, JIMMY. IT'S A REAL DRAG, MAN. DON'T EVER TAKE YOUR HEALTH FOR GRANTED, SON. HEY HOW'S YOUR MOM DOING?

BOY, WHEN I GO IT'S GONNA BE LIKE THE OLD INDIANS - JUST WANDER OFF INTO THE WOODS.

SHE'S IN AND OUT OF THE HOSPITAL BUT GETTIN' AROUND.

JEEZ I HOPE NOT!

I WATCHED HIM EAT A CHIP, HIS FINGERNAILS THICK AND GRAY. I IMAGINED THEM PLUCKING BASS STRINGS, STRONG AND DELICATE LIKE AGILE IRON.

NO HOSPITALS FOR ME, MAN.

I AIN'T GOIN' OUT LIKE THAT.

OK, POP.

ANYWAY I AIN'T GOIN' ANYWHERE SOON, PUNK - YOU'RE STUCK WITH ME.

SOUNDS GOOD.

YOU KNOW JIMMY, IT'S ALWAYS A REAL PRESSURE - I MEAN PLEASURE - HANGIN' OUT WITH YOU. HA HA HA HA

NEVER GETS OLD, POP.

HA HA HA

YEAH MAN

HE NEVER CAME INTO THE HOUSE SO I SAW HIM TO HIS CAR. A SADNESS DRAINED ME AS HE DROVE AWAY - MY FATHER! HE WAS HUMAN AND WOULD ONE DAY LEAVE AND I WASN'T READY.

I RECALLED HITTING A *JAZZ* CLUB DOWNTOWN WITH HIM—HE WAS SOBER, I WASN'T. LOOKING BACK, I REALIZED THAT HE WAS *TRYING*.

THIS PLACE AIN'T WHAT IT USED TO BE BUT ALL THE JOINTS ARE *DYIN' OUT*.

HUH.

DON'T GET WEIRD IN HERE, OK?

WE SAT QUIETLY IN THE BACK AND ORDERED FOOD. I WATCHED THE *TRIO* BUT SOON ENOUGH I WAS WATCHING *HIM* WATCH THE TRIO. HE WAS *INTO* IT.

YEAH, MAN.

NOT JUST INTO IT, HE WAS *LOST* IN IT. LOST IN THE ECSTASY OF THE MUSIC AND THE *SCENE*.

HE LOVED BEING IN *NATURE*. HE WAS CALMEST THEN... BUT IT WAS ONLY IN MUSIC THAT HE FOUND THAT JOY, I BELIEVE. ONLY IN THE MUSIC.

YEAH, MAN! WHAT DO YOU THINK OF *THAT*, JIMMY?

PRETTY GOOD!

"PRETTY GOOD." C'MON MAN, DON'T BE SQUARE, SAY "FAR OUT"!

UGH... FAR OUT.

YEAH! HA HA HA HA

A *SINGER* CAME OUT FOR A FEW TUNES, THEN PEERED OUT INTO THE CROWD.

I HEARD WE HAVE AN OLD FRIEND OUT THERE... WHERE ARE YOU, BILLY?

I SEE YOU.

FOLKS, LET'S GET HIM UP HERE. PUT YOUR HANDS TOGETHER FOR BILL TERRY.

NO, NO

COME ON, BILL.

CLAP CLAP CLAP

HE ACTED LIKE HE DIDN'T WANT TO GO UP AND PLAY FOR ABOUT *FIVE SECONDS* BEFORE SPRINGING OUT OF HIS SEAT. I TRIED NOT TO SMILE AT HIS EXCITEMENT.

CLAP CLAP CLAP

SORRY, JIMMY. I GOTTA GO DO THIS REAL QUICK.

HA HA, OKAY, POP. FAR OUT.

AS HE STEPPED IN AND STARTED TO PLAY I REALIZED I'D NEVER SEEN HIM WITH EVERYTHING ELSE SCRAPED AWAY AND IN HIS MOST NATURAL STATE.

HE WAS MUSIC. A SYMPHONY, A CACOPHONY. A SOLO AND A CODA.

THE MOMENT WAS FLEETING, WE'D FIGHT AGAIN LATER.

BUT I WOULD NEVER FORGET IT.

I STAYED WITH HIM THE NEXT COUPLE DAYS, GOING HOME AT NIGHT. HE WAS IN *BAD SHAPE* BUT REFUSED TO GO TO THE HOSPITAL, STAYING IN BED MOSTLY.

WHAT'RE YOU LOOKING AT, INDIO?

JUST THE BACK YARD, ALL THE TREES YOU PLANTED.

MEMORIAS. THOSE TREES, THEY'LL JUST *BULLDOZE* 'EM WHEN I'M GONE, MAN.

...

IT'S THE CYCLE OF LIFE, JIMMY.

NOBODY SHOULD STICK AROUND FOREVER, MAN.

I'M PROUD OF YOU KIDS.

YOU AND YOUR SISTER, YA GOTTA *STICK TOGETHER.*

PROMISE ME, SON.

ALWAYS, POP.

YOU'RE A GOOD SON.

A *WEIRD DUDE,* BUT A GOOD SON.

NOW GO HOME, MAN. YOU'RE *CRAMPIN'* MY STYLE.

YOU'LL COME BACK TOMORROW, YEAH?

I'LL BE HERE. FIRST THING.

I DROVE HIS TRUCK HOME AND CHECKED MY PHONE EVERY FIVE MINUTES—NO MESSAGE FROM HIM. NONE WHEN I AWOKE AT SIX. I HEADED OUT.

HOPEFULLY HE JUST SLEPT WELL.

YOU DON'T BELIEVE THAT.

OH GOD.

ELENA WAS ALREADY DRIVING DOWN—WE HAD DECIDED TO *FORCE* HIM INTO THE HOSPITAL THAT MORNING, AGAINST HIS *WILL* IF NEED BE.

I KNEW. THE SECOND I OPENED THE DOOR I KNEW.

THE HOUSE WAS EMPTY.

POP?

HIS BODY WAS THERE, BUT DAD WAS GONE.

NO.

I DID MY BEST TO CLEAN HIM UP BEFORE ELENA ARRIVED.

I THANKED HIM. I SAT WITH HIM AND THANKED HIM FOR TAKING US TO THE **COUNTRY** AND THE **CITY** AND FOR WHISTLING IN THE KITCHEN WHILE HE COOKED FOOD FOR US TO EAT SO WE'D **KNOW** —

—SO WE'D KNOW HE WAS THERE.

AND HE WAS ALWAYS THERE

WE **FOUGHT** BECAUSE WE WERE TOO MUCH OF THE SAME KIND BUT HE WAS ALWAYS THERE.

FOR ELENA.

FOR ME.

I THANKED HIM AND I WAITED FOR MY SISTER TO COME HOME.

THERE IS NO RIGHT WAY TO GRIEVE. WE ALL CARRY THE BURDEN OUR OWN WAY AND I CRAMMED MY GRIEF DOWN LOW.

HE WENT OUT THE WAY HE WANTED. HE SAID HIS PIECE AND SET HIS THINGS IN ORDER AND STAYED THE HELL OUT OF THE HOSPITAL WITH THEIR "TUBES AND MACHINES", AS HE PUT IT.

MOM SHOWED UP WITH HER BROTHERS AND SISTERS AND THEIR SORROW WAS GENUINE. BILL STAYED PART OF THE FAMILY. HE DROVE UP TO THE DELLS WITH THE LAWNMOWER IN THE TRUCK SO HE COULD MOW KUNIKA'S LAWN. HE TOOK ALL THOSE KIDS ON AS HIS OWN. HE WAS BELOVED BY THEM AND THIS DISCOVERY MADE MY HEART SWELL.

I LEANED ON ELENA, MY FRIENDS, AND THE THINGS I'D LEARED IN THE PROGRAM.

DEAN CAME OUT OF THE WOODWORK FOR THE FUNERAL, AS DID MANY FRIENDS. WE BURIED HIM ON A FROZEN DECEMBER DAY.

I WAS NOT ANGRY AT GOD, WASN'T ANGRY AT POP. I WAS GRATEFUL WE'D PARTED AS FATHER AND SON. ON GOOD TERMS. WITH LOVE.

HE WAS AT REST NOW WITH HIS MOTHER AND FATHER. AND HIS BROTHERS. JAMES, BOBBY, AND TOMMY.

ELENA AND I WERE THE LAST.

THE THINGS THEY *LEAVE BEHIND*.

WALLETS WITH MONEY THEY'D NEVER SPEND AND PHOTOS *TREASURED*, HIDDEN AWAY.

A SOBRIETY COIN.

A DOG-EARED BUSINESS CARD WITH THE SCRAWLED, HANDWRITTEN NOTE ON THE BACK: "IN EVENT OF INJURY, SICKNESS, OR DEATH CONTACT MY SON JAMES TERRY" WITH MY PHONE NUMBER ON THERE.

LOVE LETTERS

PHOTO ALBUMS

OUR OLD REPORT CARDS

TEACHINGS OF THE BUDDHA WITH HAND-WRITTEN NOTES.

A TATTERED SPANISH/ENGLISH DICTIONARY.

JIM, HE KEPT A PICTURE OF ZOE WITH HIM.

ALWAYS.

THE PLATES ON WHICH WE ATE THE FOOD HE MADE.

CHINESE FOOD LEFTOVERS HE COULDN'T STOMACH.

HIS COFFEE CUP.

AN OLD BROOM.

JUST OBJECTS.

GOODWILL

TALISMANS NOW, ALL. THERE WAS *ENERGY* IN THEM FOREVER.

MEMORIAS.

THE NOTCHES HE MADE ON THE WOODEN BEAM IN THE KITCHEN, TO MARK OUR GROWTH.

I FOUND HIS RECORD COLLECTION IN A CLOSET. JAZZ ALBUMS FROM 1962, MOSTLY. THE YEAR HE TURNED EIGHTEEN.

CARE IF I KEEP THESE?

NO. YOU SHOULD.

MINGUS

HIS INSTRUMENTS.

SILENT NOW.

SOMEHOW HIS *CLOTHES* WERE THE HARDEST, ESPECIALLY THE *SHOES*. DRESS SHOES FOR *GIGS*, GYM SHOES FOR HIKES AND YARDWORK ...HIS *BOOTS*, SO WORN.

HE WAS NOT VAIN, ALL THOSE SHOES WERE UTILITARIAN AND I IMAGINED HIM WEIGHING THEM IN HIS HANDS, PLACING THEM ON THE COUNTER.

"I'LL GET A LOT OF USE OUT OF THESE."

FOR A FEW MONTHS AFTER THE OLD MAN WAS GONE I'D DRIVE OUT TO HIS PLACE TO MOW THE LAWN, TAKE CARE OF THINGS A LITTLE.
AFTERWARD I'D SIT IN THE BACKYARD AND LOOK AT THE TREES HE'D PLANTED, LISTEN TO THE BIRDS AND WATCH THE SQUIRRELS GET BRAVE. "HE DID ALL THIS," I'D THINK. "HE GAVE THEM THIS PLACE TO BE, AND SOON IT WILL ALL BE GONE."
THE IDEA CAME TO ME THAT I'D JUST MOVE IN, HELL WITH IT. IF IT CAME TO ME LIVING ALONE, SO BE IT.

I THOUGHT, "I SHOULD CALL POP, SEE WHAT HE THINKS."

A MOMENT LATER I REMEMBERED THAT OF COURSE I COULDN'T, EVER AGAIN. HE WAS GONE. GRANDMA AND GRANDPA. CHOKA, KUNIKA... THEY WERE JUST... GONE. **DON** WAS GONE.

WHO WOULD I ASK FOR ADVICE? THE WORLD STRETCHED AND CONTRACTED BEFORE ME LIKE VERTIGO AND THE VERY NATURE OF TIME AND MORTALITY - FREEDOM AND FEAR - FELL ON ME LIKE SUDDEN NIGHT.

LESS THAN A YEAR LATER IT WAS MOM. SHE WAS RACED TO THE HOSPITAL IN MADISON - I DROVE UP.

JIM...IT'S TOO MUCH. TOO SOON.

I KNOW. I KNOW.

THE **LUPUS, DIABETES,** HER **LIVER**... IT WAS ALL HITTING AT ONCE. SHE WAS IN A COMA.

MEGAN, ELENA, AND I WERE PUT IN CHARGE OF HER OUTCOME.

HER BODY WAS GIVING UP.

FRANKLY IT'S AMAZING SHE'S BEEN WITH US AS LONG AS SHE HAS.

YEAH. THANKS.

THAT WAITING ROOM WAS A PURGATORY, BUT THERE WAS STILL LAUGHTER. HER BROTHERS AND SISTERS AND ALL WHO'S LIVES SHE TOUCHED CAME TO SEE HER AND PRAY.

ZOE, GO GET YOU AND YOUR BROTHERS SOMETHING TO EAT.

JEEZ, YOUR MOM EVER TELL YOU 'BOUT THE TIME WE GOT ALL MESSED UP AND RODE FROM...

OK. MOM.

THE MEN DISTRACTED THEMSELVES WITH TALK OF SPORTS OR POLITICS WHILE THE WOMEN TOOK CARE OF EVERYTHING. I AM TOLD THIS DIVISION OF DUTIES IS A RESULT OF COLONIAL INFLUENCE - BUT THE WOMEN IN MY FAMILY ALWAYS FELT STRONGER TO ME.

HEY MOM...

...ANYTHING I CAN DO?

THANK YOU, J.T.

CAN YOU RUN OUT AND PICK UP SOME MORE SANDWICH FIXIN'S, SON?

ELENA TOOK CARE OF DAD'S AFFAIRS WHEN HE LEFT AND WAS NOW SHOULDERING THIS. THE WOMEN HAVE ALWAYS BEEN THE SPINE. I FELT LIKE AN ARM... OCCASIONALLY USEFUL.

I THINK WE CALLED EVERYONE... I NEED TO GET IN TOUCH WITH HER INSURANCE... DO WE NEED TO GET MORE FOOD?

HEIDI'S MAKING FOOD AND SAMANTHA BROUGHT STUFF... THERESA AND I CAN HIT COSTCO, GET GAMES FOR THE KIDS-

GOTTA CALL THE TRIBE...

OUT OF NOWHERE MOM FOUGHT HER WAY BACK AND WE WERE OVERJOYED. SOON SHE WAS LAUGHING AND JOKING. SHE TALKED TO US.

HI, MOM.

OH, MY BABIES. I LOVE YOU GUYS. WHO'S GONNA GO GET ME A SONIC BURGER? THE FOOD HERE SUCKS!

HA HA OH JEEZ.

BINGO AND BURGERS AWAIT YOU ON THE OUTSIDE, MA!

THEY RECOMMENDED TRANSFER OUT OF *ICU* AND SO WE *DID*. I VISITED HER IN THE NEW FACILITY— HER DECLINE WAS ALMOST *IMMEDIATE*.

DID WE MAKE A *MISTAKE*?

GODDAMN DOCTORS. THEY JUST PRETEND TO KNOW! DAD HAD THE RIGHT IDEA!

I'M SO SORRY, MOM...

SHE STOPPED *BREATHING* AND WENT BACK TO THE *ICU*.

WE CANNOT GUARANTEE THAT SHE WILL COME OUT OF THE COMA... OR THAT SHE WILL BREATHE ON HER OWN AGAIN.

WE ARE, HOWEVER, ALMOST CERTAIN SHE WILL NOT BE THE SAME IF SHE DOES.

THE LIKELIHOOD OF HER WAKING UP OR... HAVING ANY FUNCTIONS IS... ALMOST NONE.

I'M SORRY... BUT YOU HAVE A DIFFICULT DECISION TO MAKE.

THERE WAS NONE TO BE MADE. SHE'D BEEN VERY *CLEAR* THAT SHE HAD NO WISH TO BE KEPT ALIVE UNDER THESE CONDITIONS.

WE HAD TO LET HER GO.

SOME OF THE FAMILY *FOUGHT* US ON THIS. I WAS STUNNED. THEN I WAS *ANGRY*. SO ANGRY.

JIM... KUNIKA TOLD ME WE'RE SUPPOSED TO BE JOYFUL THAT SHE'S ON THE NEXT JOURNEY.

IF WE'RE FIGHTING THE NATURAL ORDER... IF WE ARE UNWILLING TO LET GO IT'S BECAUSE WE FEEL GUILTY ABOUT HOW WE *LEFT* THINGS. I MADE *PEACE* WITH MOM, YOU DID TOO.

DON'T LET THEM GET TO YOU.

WE WENT INTO THE ROOM WITH HER AS THEY UNPLUGGED ALL THE MACHINES. WE TALKED TO HER, HOLDING HER SOFT HANDS AS SHE STRUGGLED TO BREATHE.

WE TOLD HER NOT TO *WORRY* ABOUT US, THAT SHE WOULD SEE *TONY* ON HER NEXT JOURNEY. SHE NEVER WOKE UP. SHE JUST STOPPED *STRUGGLING*.

WE STAYED WITH HER AS LONG AS WE COULD. MOM WAS FINALLY AT PEACE BUT I WAS RIPPED TO SHREDS.

SHE WENT ON HER JOURNEY IN THE TRADITIONAL *HO-CHUNK* WAY WITH A FOUR-DAY *CEREMONY*.

MY BROTHERS AND SISTERS STEPPED UP. I MET FAMILY I DIDN'T KNOW I HAD AND THEY TOOK CARE OF EVERYTHING.

I FELT THE EMBRACE OF THE *TRIBE*, OF THE *OLD WAYS*, FOR THE FIRST TIME AS THEY GUIDED ME THROUGH WHAT HAD TO BE *DONE*.

ON THE FOURTH DAY MOM LEFT US WITH THE *SUNRISE* FOR HER *NEXT JOURNEY*.

I SANK INTO A BIT OF A DEPRESSION BUT DUG MY HEELS IN AND CLUNG TO MY ROUTINE.

BARELY DREW TODAY. DON'T KNOW WHERE THE NEXT GIG IS COMING FROM... WHAT'S THE POINT.

GUESS I'LL GO TO THE MEETING.

HOW'RE THINGS GOING, LAD? YOU BEEN OKAY?

EH, I'M FINE.

YOU'VE BEEN THROUGH A BIT, IT'S OKAY TO-

I'M FINE.

OKAY THEN, FUCKER, YER FINE!!

I GOT IT IN MY HEAD THAT MY GRIEF WAS BELLYACHING AND THAT NOBODY WANTED TO BE BOTHERED BY IT.

DON'T BUG YOUR SPONSOR, YOU JUST WHINE ABOUT THE SAME GARBAGE OVER AND OVER.

AS THAT ONE ASSHOLE SAID, "GET OVER IT."

YA JERK. YA LOSER.

JUST DEAL WITH IT...

MY BRAIN WAS TRYING TO CONVINCE ME THAT I WAS UTTERLY ALONE. IT WAS GIVING ME REASONS-

HOW DO YOU KNOW YOU WERE EVER REALLY LOVED? BECAUSE SOMEONE SAID THOSE WORDS? THEY COULD LIE...

...ESPECIALLY IF THEY HATE YOU. THEN THE LIE IS TWICE AS SWEET! FRIENDSHIP COULD BE A LIE AS WELL...

- REASONS TO DRINK.

MY REASONABLE MIND UNDERSTOOD THAT THE MORE ALONE I FELT THE CLOSER TO A DRINK I WAS. MY ALCOHOLIC BRAIN WANTED NOTHING MORE.

CRIPES, MAN YOU'VE BEEN GOING TO THESE THREE TIMES A WEEK FOR OVER TEN YEARS!

YOU'RE STILL AS ALONE AS EVER! YOU COULD DIE TOMORROW AND NOBODY HERE WOULD BAT AN EYE!

YOU CHUMP.

I WAS HITTING WHAT IS REFERRED TO AS A SOBER BOTTOM. I WAS STAYING SOBER BUT MY HEAD HAD TAKEN THE BALL AND WAS RUNNING WITH IT. FEAR WAS SNEAKING IN - OVER LOVE, FINANCES, CLIMATE CHANGE, GLOBAL DESTRUCTION - EVERYTHING. DESPAIR AND HOPELESSNESS SNUCK IN WITH IT.

JUST DON'T ACT ON THIS CRAZINESS!

JUST DON'T FORGET, THIS FEELING IS NOT FOREVER.

YOUR HEAD IS TRYING TO KILL YOU, SUCKA.

YOU'VE BEEN HERE BEFORE.

YOU CAN OUTLAST THE BASTARD.

LITTLE RUMBLINGS ON SOCIAL MEDIA ABOUT AN OIL PIPELINE DISPUTE CAUGHT MY ATTENTION. I BEGAN TO FOLLOW WHAT WAS GOING DOWN.

THE HELL'S GOIN' ON HERE? BUNCHA *NATIVES* TRYIN' TO STOP THE OIL EMPIRE?

A 'HO! GOOD LUCK, GUYS. IT'S A LOST CAUSE BUT I'LL TIP MY HAT TO YOU.

I COULDN'T GET IT OUT OF MY HEAD. I FOUND OUT WHAT I *COULD* ABOUT WHAT WAS HAPPENING.

THIS PIPELINE, WHICH IRONICALLY STARTS ON *NATIVE* LAND, WAS SUPPOSED TO GO NEAR BISMARCK BUT THEY SAID, "FUCK NO, THAT SEEMS DANGEROUS—

"LET'S RUN IT THROUGH THE *REZ* BECAUSE FUCK THEM ANYWAY."

REALLY? FAHK.

YEAH, I KNOW.

AS IF THAT WEREN'T SHITTY ENOUGH THEY WANT TO PUT IT UNDER AN *AQUIFER*, WHICH SUPPLIES MOST OF THE MIDWEST'S WATER!

PIPELINES *SPILL*— IT'S WHAT THEY DO! I DON'T GET IT. AND THE OIL ISN'T EVEN FOR AMERICA! IT'S EXPORT OIL SO NO JOBS, NO CHEAPER GAS, JUST MORE MONEY FOR THE RICH!

YEAH... THAT'S DUMB.

EXPLAIN TO ME HOW PLOWING THROUGH SACRED BURIAL GROUNDS ISN'T *ILLEGAL*? IF IT WAS A DAMN CEMETERY—

CEMETERY'S PRIVATE PROPERTY...

THEN HONOR THE *TREATIES*, RIGHT?

HA HA— *RIGHT.*

UGH.

I STARTED SENDING SUPPLIES VIA ONLINE STORES BUT EVERYTHING WAS CONFUSING. NEWS WAS SCANT.

ELENA, I WANT TO HELP BUT I MAY AS WELL BE SENDING THAT STUFF TO OUTER SPACE.

THEY'RE SICCING DOGS ON THEM... DROPPING *CHEMICALS* FROM HELICOPTERS, SHOOTING THEM WITH RUBBER BULLETS... GOD. AND NONE OF THESE POLITICIANS OR "NEWS" OUTLETS EVEN HAVE THE BALLS TO MENTION IT!

ONE NIGHT I WATCHED A *LIVE FEED* OF POLICE, NATIONAL GUARD, AND HIRED MERCENARIES SPRAY RESISTERS WITH WATER HOSES IN SUB-ZERO TEMPERATURES. A WOMAN'S ARM WAS NEARLY SEVERED BY AN EXPLODING GAS CANNISTER. I WAS *SICK TO MY STOMACH* ABOUT IT ALL.

I DON'T KNOW, 'LENA. I THINK I GOTTA GO.

LET'S GO THEN. COME UP TO THE DELLS AND WE'LL GO TOGETHER.

I PACKED A FEW THINGS AND HEADED TO THE **DELLS**. ELENA WAS GETTING DONATIONS TOGETHER AND EVERYONE WANTED TO HELP.

ALL THE NATIONS WERE **COMING TOGETHER**. **COMANCHES** WERE DRIVING FIREWOOD UP THERE. DINÉ AND MOHAWK AND ALGONQUIN AND OTHERS I'D ONLY **READ** ABOUT... JOURNEYING.

IT WASN'T JUST NATIVES, EITHER. ANYONE WHO CARED ABOUT THE PLANET OR WHAT KIND OF WORLD WE WERE LEAVING FOR THE **NEXT GENERATION** WAS **WELCOME**.

WHY **NOT** THIS URBAN NATIVE? THIS HALF-BREED WHO NEVER FELT HE BELONGED ANYWHERE OR WITH ANY GROUP? THERE WAS **NOBODY LEFT** TO **DEFINE** ME.

HOME WAS NO LONGER WHERE IT'D ALWAYS BEEN. THEY BULL-DOZED POP'S HOUSE AND THE DELLS NO LONGER MEANT **MOM**.

I BEGAN THE JOURNEY UPSET AND **LONELY**. IT DIDN'T MATTER. SOON I'D BE OFF WITH MY SISTER AND COUSIN, DOING SOMETHING.

I WAS NO BRAVE WARRIOR—MY SELF-PRESERVATION INSTINCTS KEPT ME FROM HEROICS BUT I HOPED TO HELP IN **SOME** WAY, MAYBE EVEN **LEARN** A LITTLE.

MAYBE. IF THEY'D **HAVE** ME.

PART 5

WETHA, ELENA, AND I PACKED THE JEEP WITH ANYTHING WE COULD THINK TO BRING. THERE WERE BLANKETS AND JACKETS AND **COLD WEATHER** GEAR. WE PLANNED ON SLEEPING IN A *TENT* BUT REALLY HAD NO IDEA WHAT TO EXPECT.

MANNY, WETHA'S SON, MADE HER PROMISE **NOT** TO GET ARRESTED. "BUT THIS IS FOR *MOTHER NATURE*, SON." SHE REASONED. "YEAH, BUT YOU'RE *MY* MOTHER." SO SHE PROMISED HIM.

I WAS GOING WITH TWO OF MY FAVORITE PEOPLE BUT I WAS STILL NERVOUS. SURE, I WAS WORRIED ABOUT THE *PHYSICAL DANGER* — THE VIDEOS SHOWED CLEAR *HARMFUL INTENT* AND I UNDERSTOOD THAT THE "NON-LETHAL" AMMO WAS SPECIFICALLY BEING AIMED AT *FACES* AND *GROINS*. *DIRTY POKER* AND *PAINFUL*. *CRIPPLING* PAINFUL. TERRIFYING.

WHAT WORRIED ME MORE WAS THAT - UNLIKE ME - THESE WERE REAL INDIANS. NATIVES WHO WERE TAKING A STAND AGAINST SOMETHING OLDER THAN THE COUNTRY ITSELF ~ GREED... TO PROTECT A RESOURCE AS OLD AS LIFE ~ WATER ...

WOULD THEY SPOT ME AS A FRAUD IMMEDIATELY? WOULD THEY KNOW THAT - ALTHOUGH MY INTENTIONS WERE TRUE - I WAS NOT QUALIFIED TO STAND ALONGSIDE THEM? THE LIFELONG FEELING OF EXCLUSION, A GENETICALLY INDUCED IMPOSTER SYNDROME RATTLED AT THE BACK OF MY MIND AND IN THE BASE OF MY GUT.

I TUCKED IT DEEP DOWN AND WE ROLLED OUT OF THE DELLS.

LONG STRETCHES OF ROAD AND THE GPS WAS HILARIOUSLY INEPT. WE WORRIED MAYBE WE WERE ON THE WRONG STRETCH WHEN AN *EAGLE* SOARED ABOVE US.

"NO, WE'RE ON THE RIGHT ROAD."

WE LAUGHED A LITTLE AT THAT, THEN WENT QUIET BECAUSE WE ALL BELIEVED IT WAS TRUE.

WE WERE TREATED TO A PRETTY SPECTACULAR MINNESOTA SUNSET AS WE PASSED THE CITY. WETHA USED TO LIVE THERE AND WE STOPPED TO EAT AT ONE OF HER OLD HAUNTS, AND I PONDERED HOW LITTLE I KEPT UP WITH MY FAMILY. SHE WENT THROUGH SOME REAL HARD TIMES TO GET TO THIS MOMENT, SAME AS ELENA DID. SAME AS ME, I SUPPOSED.

AND SO HERE WERE THREE NATIVES ALIVE IN THIS WORLD. OUR ANCESTORS WERE HUNTED AND KILLED (OR IMPRISONED IN ONE WAY OR ANOTHER) BY THE VERY GOVERNMENT WE THREE LIVED UNDER. ALCOHOL AND STRANGE, UNHEALTHY FOOD TRIED TO KILL US AS DID EVERY TEACHER, MOVIE, BOOK, AND POLITICIAN THAT TRIED TO TELL US WE WERE NO LONGER RELEVANT.

WE THREE WHO STUMBLED THROUGH THIS WORLD AND MADE MISTAKES AND STRUGGLED TO FIGURE WHERE WE FIT IN—WHERE WE *BELONGED*... WERE TOGETHER *NOW* IN A JEEP ON THE WAY TO THE BIGGEST INDIGENOUS RESISTANCE IN RECENT HISTORY.

WE WERE *RIGHT* WHERE WE BELONGED.

SOMEHOW.

AS WE ROLLED IN TO SOUTH DAKOTA THE SUN VANISHED AND THE WORLD TURNED WAY DARKER THAN I WAS USED TO. GPS WAS WORTHLESS BUT WE'D SEEN AN EAGLE FLYING ALONGSIDE US EARLIER AND WE TOOK IT AS A GOOD SIGN. WHAT WASN'T A GOOD SIGN WERE THE MANY *TRUMP* SIGNS WE SAW... I HAD THE SINKING DREAD THAT HE MIGHT ACTUALLY WIN, AS INSANE AS IT SEEMED—AND HE WAS NO FRIEND TO *NATIVES* OR *NATURE*. HE ALSO HAD MONEY IN THE VERY PIPELINE IN QUESTION. I PUSHED IT DOWN—OUT OF MY HANDS.

AFTER A WHILE IT WAS AS IF WE WERE ON A DISTANT PLANET, THERE WAS *NO LIGHT* SAVE OURS AND THE WORLD SEEMED TO END JUST BEYOND THE HEADLIGHTS. ELENA PUT IN *NEIL YOUNG* AND IT WAS A COMFORT TO US ALL.

I ASKED THEM IF THEY WERE NERVOUS.

ELENA BELIEVED IN WHAT WAS HAPPENING THERE AND SAW IT AS THE BEAUTIFUL, IMPORTANT THING IT WAS... WHICH PUT HER FEARS WAY IN THE BACKGROUND.

WETHA WAS EXCITED—TO BE THERE, TO HOPEFULLY SEE FAMILY AND FRIENDS SHE *HADN'T* FOR SOME TIME... AND TO FIGHT THE MAN IN WHATEVER WAY SHE COULD.

ME, I WAS BEGINNING TO WONDER WHY I WAS ALONG. I KEPT THAT TO MYSELF.

WE DROVE DEEPER INTO THE DARKNESS AND IT HIT ME OUT OF NOWHERE HOW *ALONE* WE THREE WERE. *ALL* OF OUR PARENTS WERE GONE. WETHA'S FATHER, AN ACTIVIST AND BADASS, HAD PASSED SOME TIME BEFORE AND HER MOTHER, JEAN - A LEGENDARY ACTIVIST AND ONE OF THE STRONGEST WOMEN I KNEW - WENT BACK TO THE EARTH JUST RECENTLY.

AND OF COURSE ... ELENA AND I WERE ALONE NOW.

WE FELT AS THOUGH THE SPIRIT OF JEAN DAY WAS CHEERING US ON. MOM WOULD HAVE BEEN WORRIED ABOUT US. DAD? HE PROBABLY WOULD HAVE THOUGHT WE WERE *NUTS.*

BUT THEY WERE *GONE* NOW. THE MANY TIMES I THOUGHT OF CALLING THEM ONLY TO *PAUSE* AND REMEMBER. WE WERE BEHOLDEN TO NO ONE SAVE THE *NEXT GENERATION* AND THERE WASN'T ANYONE FOR US TO ASK "HOW SHOULD WE PROCEED?" IN THAT DARKNESS I BEGAN TO UNDERSTAND THE IDEA OF LIVING FOR THE *NEXT GENERATION.* THOSE WHO CAME BEFORE LEAVE, AND SOMETIMES THEY LEAVE A MESS. SOMETIMES THEY PREPARE YOU AND SOMETIMES THEY CRIPPLE YOU BUT IN THE END IT'S UP TO YOU HOW YOU LIVE AND THE ONES WHO *BENEFIT* OR *SUFFER* ARE THE *CHILDREN WE HAVE NOW.*

I THINK EVERYONE WHO WAS RESISTING AT STANDING ROCK UNDERSTOOD THAT *LONG* BEFORE I DID.

I STILL DON'T *COMPLETELY* UNDERSTAND, BUT I'M TRYING.

WE CROSSED INTO *NORTH DAKOTA* AND THE AIR CHANGED.
THERE WAS TENSION IN THE FACES AT THE GAS STATIONS
AND TO A DEGREE IT FELT LIKE IT WAS ALIVE IN THE DARKNESS.

WE STOPPED AT THE CASINO GAS STATION AND FUELED
UP AND THERE WAS A STRAIN. IT WAS GOOD TO SEE
NATIVES BUT THEY SEEMED TIRED AND SUSPICIOUS.

ON THE ROAD IN WE PASSED SEVERAL BLACK HUMVEES
AND WHAT SEEMED TO BE A *MOBILE SURVEILLANCE TRUCK*.
I'D READ OF TRAVELLERS BEING STOPPED BY THE POLICE
AND SEARCHED OR DETAINED. WE HELD OUR BREATH
AND *CONTINUED*.

THERE WAS A PILE ON THE SIDE OF THE ROAD THAT LOOKED
LIKE IMPORTANT PERSONAL BELONGINGS. WE WERE TOLD
LATER THAT THEY WERE *SPIRITUAL ARTIFACTS* THAT'D BEEN
TAKEN DURING A RAID, SPIT AND URINATED UPON, THEN
DUMPED ON THE SHOULDER.

EVENTUALLY WE BEGAN TO SEE LIGHTS. I'D NEVER FELT LIKE MORE OF A *TOURIST* AS WE DROVE THROUGH THE REZ. THE DARK SLEEPING HOMES OF THOSE WHO DEALT WITH THIS HOSTILITY AND OPPRESSION *EVERY DAY*. I BRISTLED AT THE IDEA OF ANY MODERN *NON-NATIVE* BEING RELOCATED AGAINST THEIR WILL AND TOLD "THIS IS WHERE YOU LIVE NOW."

THERE WERE A FEW DIFFERENT CAMPS AND WE ENDED UP AT THE LARGEST ONE, OCETI. SOMEONE MANNING THE GATE STEPPED UP AND ASKED IF WE WERE CARRYING ANY DRUGS, ALCOHOL, OR WEAPONS. WE SAID NO.

HERE, I THOUGHT, WAS WHERE I'D BE EXPOSED. YOU CAN'T COME IN HERE, FAKER, YOU'RE BARELY NATIVE. THANKS FOR YOUR CHEAP IDEALISM BUT YOU HAVEN'T EARNED THE RIGHT TO BE HERE.

HE LOOKED IN THE JEEP. "THIS YOUR FIRST TIME AT THE CAMP?"

WE TOLD HIM IT WAS AND HE SMILED AND SAID,

"WELCOME HOME."

THANKING HIM, WE ROLLED ON THROUGH PAST CONSTRUCTS STURDY AND RAMSHACKLE, TENTS AND CAMPERS AND WOOD STRUCTURES AND CARS AND *TIPIS* EXTENDING INTO THE BLACK BEYOND HEADLIGHTS OR CAMPFIRES. FIGURES WANDERED IN AND OUT OF THE LIGHT AS WE IDLED THROUGH ON THE HARD-PACKED AND FROZEN MUD PATH.

FINALLY WE CAME TO A STOP ON THE OUTSKIRTS AND SET UP OUR TENT IN THE DARKNESS, WHICH WAS NOT TOTAL. ACROSS THE RIVER ON THE *DAPL* SIDE BEAMED GREAT WHITE *FLOODLIGHTS*, ILLUMINATING THE PIPELINE'S CONSTRUCTION AREA AND KEEPING AN EYE ON THE EDGE OF CAMP.

THE EERIE MECHANICAL BUZZ OF A SMALL *AIRPLANE* CIRCLED OVER THE CAMP, A DARK AND LIGHTLESS SHADOW BLOTTING OUT THE STARS AS WE SETTLED IN. OUR PHONES WERE FUNCTIONING ODDLY, MINE HAD THE WRONG DATE AND TIME. I WAS TOLD LATER THAT THE PLANE HAD SOME KIND OF SCRAMBLER ON IT.

NAZGUL, I THOUGHT. THOSE FLOODLIGHTS ARE THE EYE OF SAURON AND WE'RE ALL ON THE EDGE OF MORDOR.

THE COLD SNAPPED ME OUT OF NERD LAND AND BACK TO THE ACTUAL SITUATION. I WORRIED ABOUT MY CATS BACK HOME. HOW BITTER I WAS THAT I'D FOUGHT WITH SOMEONE DEAR TO ME BEFORE I'D LEFT.

IT ALL SEEMED VERY FAR AWAY NOW AND THE COLD WAS RIDICULOUS.

WE AGREED THAT A TRIP TO BISMARCK FOR WARMER GEAR WAS IN ORDER AND I TRIED TO FIGURE A WAY TO COMPLETELY COVER MY FACE AND STILL BREATHE. BEFORE I FINALLY DRIFTED OFF TO AN UNEASY SLEEP I SHOT OUT MY USUAL PRAYER TO OL' H.P., MY "HIGHER POWER."

THANK YOU FOR KEEPING ME SOBER TODAY. THANK YOU FOR THE DAY. THANK YOU FOR MY FAMILY AND FRIENDS. PLEASE HELP ME TO DO MORE GOOD THAN HARM. AND... LET ME BE OF SOME SERVICE HERE... THIS SITUATION SUCKS.

WE WALKED AROUND A BIT THE FIRST NIGHT BUT WERE TRIPPING OVER TENT ROPES AND STUMBLING INTO DEAD ENDS. THE NEXT MORNING I WOKE UP BEFORE THE SUN, STIFF AND COLD AND IN NEED OF COFFEE. I GRABBED MY CUP AND HEADED INTO THE CHILL DARKNESS.

I MET A FELLA FROM OREGON WHO WAS MANNING A LARGE COFFEE MACHINE. HE'D BEEN THERE FOR WEEKS AND HE EXPLAINED THE GENERAL AIR OF THE CAMP, LAUGHING WHEN I OFFERED TO PAY FOR THE COFFEE. HE TOLD ME THAT AT DAWN AN ELDER SPOKE AT THE *SACRED FIRE* AND I SHOULD CHECK IT OUT FOR A MORE ACCURATE GAUGE.

AFTER FINDING OUT WHERE TO DONATE THE *GEAR* WE BROUGHT I FOLLOWED A PATH TO THE SACRED FIRE. I FOUND A SPOT TO *LEAN* AND AS THE SUN CAME UP THE P.A. SYSTEM CRACKLED TO LIFE AS THE ELDER BEGAN TO PRAY. IT WAS IN *LAKOTA* SO I DIDN'T FOLLOW, BUT IT WAS NICE TO HEAR THE LANGUAGE BEING SPOKEN. AFTER THE PRAYER HE GREETED US IN ENGLISH.

HE SPOKE OF THE URGENCY OF THE RESISTANCE, AND THE IMPORTANCE OF *PEACEFUL ACTS* - THE DANGER OF BEING GOADED INTO REACTION. PATIENCE AND A *SPIRITUAL STRENGTH* WERE ALLIES. VIOLENCE WAS A TRAP THAT *DAPL* WANTED THE RESISTANCE TO FALL FOR.

BEHIND HIM WERE GREAT HILLS, SCORCHED AT THEIR PEAKS TO THE DIRT. I WAS LATER TOLD THAT A *FIRE* WAS LIT THERE AND AS IT CREPT TOWARD CAMP THERE WAS LITTLE TO DO BUT PRAY, AND A *STRONG WIND* BLEW ACROSS CAMP AND UP THE HILL - PUSHING THE FLAMES BACK TOWARD FROM WHERE THEY CAME.

I'D HEARD THAT ABOUT WHATEVER THEY WERE DUMPING FROM ABOVE WITH THEIR *HELICOPTERS*... THAT A *WIND* CAME AND BLEW IT AWAY.

I BELIEVED IT.

WHY WOULDN'T I? I'D SEEN MIRACLES HAPPEN.

IN BISMARCK WE GOT A FEEL OF THE LOCAL HOSPITALITY. IT WAS LIKE EASY RIDER WHEN WE THREE STEPPED INTO THE DINER - ELENA AND WETHA LOOKED VERY NATIVE AND ANGRY EYES FOLLOWED US TO THE BOOTH.

I UNDERSTOOD THE HOSTILITY - SOMEONE'S TRYING TO LIVE A LIFE AND THAT'S HARD ENOUGH WHEN IN COME THESE TROUBLEMAKING STRAGGLERS. THESE NATIVES WHO DON'T HAVE THE DECENCY TO DIE OUT LIKE A GOOD "CONQUERED" PEOPLE OR AT LEAST STAY PUT ON THE RESERVATIONS WHERE THEIR CONTINUING SUFFERING DOESN'T HAVE TO BE SEEN.

GOTTA COME AROUND REMINDING EVERYONE THEY'RE STILL HERE AND THAT THIS GREAT NATION WAS BUILT ON A GENOCIDE PLAN. AND NOW THEY WERE DISRUPTING THINGS, BITCHING ABOUT A PIPELINE. TALKING ABOUT THE PLANET LIKE IT WASN'T A UTILITY TO BE RAPED AND ABANDONED.

SURE, I UNDERSTOOD THE HOSTILITY.

I ALSO UNDERSTOOD WHAT THE WHITE MAN IN THE TRUMP HAT WAS DOING WHEN HE BEGAN BOASTING TO OUR VERY KIND, POSSIBLY GAY WAITER HOW THINGS WERE GOING TO CHANGE ONCE TRUMP WAS IN OFFICE.

IT WAS JUST ANOTHER BULLY. EAGER TO SHOW HIS UGLINESS, JUST WAITING TO BE TOLD IT WAS OKAY TO, LIKE A FEVERED DOG TUGGING A LEASH.

I TOLD THE WAITER HE WAS CRAZY TO LIVE UP HERE AND WE BOTH LAUGHED. WE LAUGHED LOUD ENOUGH TO BE HEARD.

WE DECIDED TO CHECK OUT THE BRIDGE, WHERE MOST OF THE ACTION TOOK PLACE. DAPL CLAIMED THE RESISTANCE SET FIRE TO SOME VEHICLES BUT THAT MADE ZERO SENSE AND WAS LAUGHED OFF BY EVERYONE AT CAMP. THE CHARRED VEHICLES WERE CLEARLY A STRATEGIC BLOCKADE TO KEEP ANYONE FROM CROSSING, AS WAS THE RAZOR WIRE STRUNG ABOUT THEM - WHICH EXTENDED OFF THE BRIDGE AND INTO THE WATER ON EITHER SIDE.

WETHA AND I WALKED TOWARD THE BRIDGE AND FOLKS WARNED US ABOUT THE SNIPERS IN THE HILLS AND ON THE VEHICLES. SHE STRODE ON CONFIDENTLY BUT I WAS SUDDENLY AWARE OF EVERY SHRUB, SOUND, AND SHIFT IN THE GENTLE BREEZE. THE SKIN ON MY FACE FELT RECEPTIVE.

WE GOT TO THE SCORCHED TRUCKS AND I NOTED THE BOILED ASPHALT AS A FEW MEN BECKONED US CLOSER. WE JOINED THEM AGAINST THE TRUCK.

"JUST STAY BEHIND THESE TRUCKS. YOU CAN PEER OVER THE SIDE IF YOU WANT BUT BE QUICK. THEY GOT PEOPLE WATCHING EVERYTHING."

I POPPED MY HEAD OVER THE HOOD AND SAW A SWAT-TYPE VEHICLE PARKED. SURE ENOUGH THERE WAS A SNIPER ON THE ROOF, AIMED RIGHT AT MY FACE. I PULLED BACK, THEN SNAPPED A PIC.

"WELL, THAT'S UNSETTLING."

"BROTHER, IT'S JUST FEAR. HE WON'T SHOOT UNLESS YOU TRY CROSSING BUT HE STAYS THERE TO KEEP YOU AFRAID."

I THOUGHT ABOUT THIS. MORE BULLIES. MORE FEAR.

HOW DOES ONE OVERCOME FEAR? FEAR USED AS A WEAPON ITSELF?

LATER ON THERE WAS AN *ENERGY SHIFT* IN THE CAMP. MOVEMENT ALL AROUND ME AND I ASKED SOMEONE AS SHE RUSHED BY WHAT WAS UP.

"IT'S A CALL TO ACTION. WE'RE GOING TO THE FRONT LINES."

"THE BRIDGE?" ~ "NO, IT'S MOVED."

"CAN I GO? CAN I FOLLOW YOU?"

SHE WAS FRUSTRATED BUT PATIENT, ASKING IF I'D *REGISTERED* YET, WHICH I HADN'T. APPARENTLY GOING TO THE LINES WAS AN ALMOST *GUARANTEED ARREST*, AND IF YOU WEREN'T IN THE CAMP'S SYSTEM THEY COULDN'T GET YOU OUT OF JAIL. THAT MEANT THE LAW COULD TRANSFER YOU SOMEWHERE VERY FAR FROM THE ACTION AND YOU MIGHT JUST GET "LOST" IN IT ALL.

I THANKED HER AND SHE NODDED, RUSHED OFF.

THE GROUND BENEATH ME TREMBLED AND I SPUN AROUND, STEPPING BACK AS THREE TEENAGE NATIVES RODE PAST ME ON HORSES, GALLOPING BAREBACK TOWARD THE FRONT LINE.

THEY DIDN'T SEE ME, THEY WERE FOCUSED ON WHERE THEY WERE HEADED AS THOUGH IT WAS TWO HUNDRED YEARS AGO AND *DEFENSE* WAS IN NEED. IT WAS 2016 AND DEFENSE WAS NEEDED. THE LAND WAS IN DANGER. THEY WANTED TO PUT SOMETHING IN THE WATER THAT COULD *KILL ALL THE LIFE* AND THEY CHARGED FORTH TO *PROTECT IT*.

WATER PROTECTORS.

I STOOD IN A DAZE, WATCHING THEM STRIDE BY. TWO BOYS AND A GIRL, NONE OF THEM MORE THAN SEVENTEEN. *FEARLESS.*

STUMBLING BACK TO OUR CAMP, PROUD OF THEM BUT ASHAMED OF MYSELF, I TOLD ELENA AND WETHA WHAT I'D LEARNED.

I WANDERED THE CAMP, TALKING TO PEOPLE AND HELPING WHERE I COULD. RUNNING INTO SOME HO-CHUNKS, I HELPED SET UP THEIR CAMP. I GOT THE SAME SILENT "TOUGH GUY" TREATMENT AND FELT PRETTY UNWELCOME SO WHEN THEY OFFERED ME SOUP I DECLINED AND WANDERED OFF AGAIN.

I CHOPPED WOOD, WHICH IS THE EASIEST THING TO DO. I HELD LADDERS, I JUST WENT FROM CAMP TO CAMP ASKING IF I COULD HELP WITH ANYTHING. MY PROGRAM OF SOBRIETY TRAINED ME - WHEN I WAS UNCOMFORTABLE, HELP. IN ANY WAY POSSIBLE. KEEPS ME BUSY AND OUT OF MY HEAD.

THE WATER PROTECTORS RETURNED, THE ACTION WAS QUICK AND NOT MUCH HAPPENED. WE'D MET WITH WETHA'S AUNT LISA, WHO WAS THERE WITH HER DAUGHTER AND A FRIEND, ALL FROM THE SOUTHEAST CHEROKEE TERRITORY. THEY WERE WARRIORS.

THEY TOLD ME THE WOMEN WERE FIRST ON THE LINES. FRONT ROW. SOME HELD LARGE MIRRORS BEFORE THEM SO THE MERCS AND POLICE COULD SEE WHAT THEY LOOKED LIKE IN THEIR GEAR, WITH THEIR WEAPONS. THE WOMEN GOT SHOT FIRST, PEPPER SPRAYED, GASSED, THEY STOOD UP FRONT.

THEY SANG AND PRAYED FOR THOSE MEN WITH WEAPONS. THAT THEY MIGHT BE ENLIGHTENED. THAT THEIR HEARTS AND MINDS MIGHT OPEN UP TO A LARGER UNDERSTANDING.

LATER, I WAS AT THE SACRED FIRE AND THERE WAS DANCING, SINGING - PRAYER. THE MAN WITH THE MIC WAS FROM THE STANDING ROCK REZ.

"THE HOSTILITY YOU'RE FEELING, THAT YOU'VE EXPERIENCED IN THE TOWNS, THAT'S HOW WE'VE ALWAYS BEEN TREATED. THEY DON'T WANT US HERE AND THEY AIN'T SHY ABOUT LETTIN' US KNOW.
BUT THAT DOESN'T MEAN WE HAVE TO LET IT POISON OUR HEARTS.
THERE'S A SNIPER LOOKING AT US RIGHT NOW. LET'S ALL WAVE TO HIM."

I WAVED IN THE GENERAL DIRECTION WITH EVERYONE ELSE, GRINNING. THEN THE MAN CONTINUED:

"LET'S WAVE TO HIM SO HE KNOWS HE'S NOT ALONE. HE'D RATHER BE WITH HIS FAMILY, NOT OUT HERE. LET HIM KNOW WE'RE HERE WITH HIM, NOT AGAINST HIM. WE ARE DOING THIS FOR HIS FAMILY, TOO."

I CONTINUED WAVING BUT MY FACE CHANGED. THIS MAN'S PHILOSOPHY PIERCED MY SPIRIT AND FILLED IT WITH LIGHT.

THAT IS HOW YOU FIGHT FEAR.

COMPASSION. EMPATHY. LOVE.

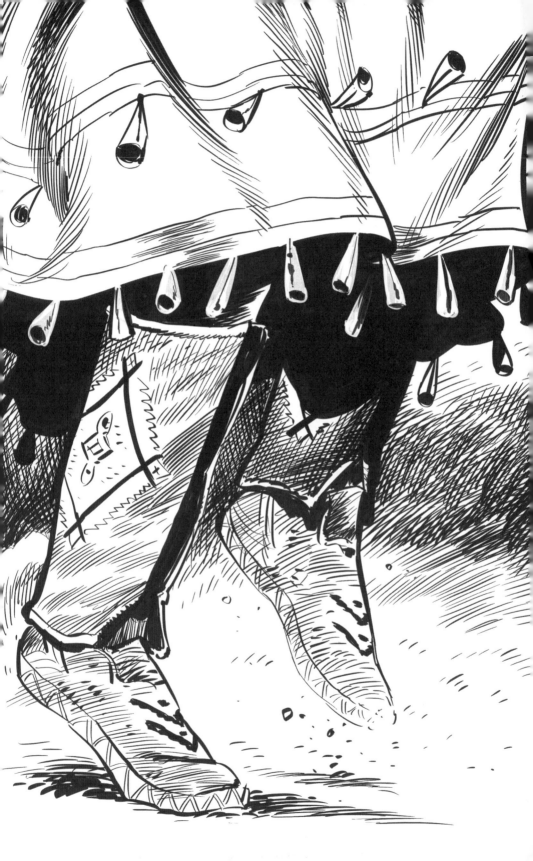

THAT IS WHAT I HEARD, THAT IS WHAT I SAW IN ACTION. OF COURSE THERE WERE THOSE WHO WANTED TO FIGHT AND THERE WAS CONFLICT BUT WHAT I SAW WAS A *PEACEFUL RESISTANCE.*

I WATCHED A WATER CEREMONY, WHICH ONLY WOMEN DO BUT ALL ARE WELCOME TO JOIN. AT THE RIVER THEY CALLED WOMEN, MEN, AND *TWO SPIRITS* TO HELP WITH THE PRAYER. THOSE WHO DIDN'T IDENTIFY AS MEN OR WOMEN, WHO WERE CONSIDERED *SACRED.*

THERE WAS A MOMENT OF PRAYER WHEN THE WOMEN RETURNED FROM A MARCH TO BRING AWARENESS TO MISSING AND MURDERED INDIGENOUS WOMEN. THE "MAN CAMPS," TEMPORARY RESIDENCIES FOR MEN WORKING THE PIPELINES, WERE NOTORIOUS BLACK HOLES FOR WOMEN, ESPECIALLY NATIVES.

PEACEFUL RESISTANCE. BUT NOT *NAIVE.* NOT *WEAK.*

AN ELDER TOOK THE MICROPHONE AND WARNED US ABOUT INFILTRATORS. LIKE *FIFTH COLUMNISTS,* THERE WERE **DAPL** FOLK WHO WERE ENTERING THE CAMP TO INCITE *VIOLENCE OR DISARRAY.* THEY WANTED THE RESISTERS TO ABANDON THE *PRAYER* AND *PICK UP GUNS.*

I'D HEARD ABOUT THIS AND I PAID ATTENTION. I WAS EAGER TO HEAR THE PLAN FOR *DEALING* WITH THIS.

"SO IF YOU SEE SOMEONE WHO'S ACTING LIKE THIS, OR SEEMS LIKE THEY DON'T BELONG..."

MY EARS BUZZED. REPORT THEM? ARE THERE POLICE OF SOME SORT?

HE CONTINUED. "IF YOU SEE SOMEONE LIKE THIS, INVITE THEM TO YOUR CAMP. TALK TO THEM. HAVE COFFEE AND FEED THEM AND LET THEM KNOW WE ARE DOING THIS FOR THEIR CHILDREN TOO."

I WAS FLOORED. I LEANED AGAINST A POLE, IT WAS ASTONISHING AND THE OPPOSITE OF HOW I'D BEEN TRAINED BY THE *CULTURE OF FEAR.*

DON'T *FEAR* YOUR NEIGHBOR. UNDERSTAND THEM.
LOVE OVER HATE.
THIS WAS *COURAGE* OF THE SPIRIT.
I WAS ELECTRIFIED.

THEY WERE THINKING.

BIGGER THAN ALL THIS.

AND THEY HAD THE HEART TO BACK IT UP.

THE NIGHT OF THE ELECTIONS I HAD TERRIBLE DREAMS. I WOKE TO COLD AND THE SOUND OF HELICOPTERS AND AIRPLANES CIRCLING ABOVE. WHEN I FINALLY AWOKE ELENA WAS SITTING UP, LOOKING AT HER PHONE.

"HE WON." SHE WHISPERED, HORRIFIED.

MY INSIDES CURDLED. SO THE CAMPAIGN OF HATE AND FEAR SPOKE TO THE PEOPLE. WE FELT SICK. THE ENTIRE CAMP HAD A GLOOM. HOPE WAS DIMINISHED. IGNORANCE AND ANGER WON... IT HARDLY SEEMED POSSIBLE. THE FUTURE FELT CLOSED. THE BULLIES HAD WON. STUNNED, WE HEADED FOR THE SACRED FIRE.

MANY WERE GATHERED, SOME WERE CRYING. THIS FIGHT WAS OVER... THE LAND WOULD NOW BE GLEEFULLY RAPED AND ABANDONED, SOLD TO THE HIGHEST BIDDER. THE RICH WOULD GET RICHER AND THE FUTURE GENERATIONS WOULD PAY THE PRICE.

AN ELDER TOOK THE MIC AND EVERYONE LISTENED, STILL IN SHOCK.

THIS IS WHAT I HEARD.

"IT'S A BAD TIME. WHEN IT'S A TIME LIKE THIS IT'S EASY TO LOSE HOPE, TO LOSE STRENGTH.

"JUST REMEMBER. TWO HUNDRED YEARS AGO THE APOCALYPSE HAPPENED FOR OUR PEOPLE, FOR THE LAND. IT WAS THE END OF ALL THINGS WHEN THE WHITE MAN CAME. THEY TOLD US ABOUT SIN. THEY TOLD US WHEN WE DIED WE'D GO TO PARADISE. BUT WE WERE ALREADY LIVING IN PARADISE.

"WHEN THEY CONVINCED US WE HAD SOULS... WE LOST OUR SPIRIT.

"BUT OUR ANCESTORS SURVIVED. THEY WERE HUNTED AND PUT IN PRISON OR KILLED. JUST FOR BEIN' INDIAN. BUT THEY SURVIVED. THEY PRAYED IN SECRET AND KEPT THE WAYS THE BEST THEY COULD.

"WE ARE THEIR GRANDCHILDREN. WE ARE HERE NOW BECAUSE THEY SURVIVED. WE ARE NOT A MYTH. WE ARE STILL HERE.

"AND OUR GRANDCHILDREN WILL BE HERE BECAUSE WE SURVIVED THESE TIMES. WE HAVE NOT LOST OUR SPIRITS. THEY WILL KNOW WE FOUGHT FOR THEM. THEY WILL BE HERE BECAUSE WE SURVIVED."

I TOOK A BREATH AND LOOKED AROUND. EVERYONE WAS HOLDING HANDS.

THEY ALL MADE ME FEEL STRONG.

NOT LONG AFTER, WE LEFT CAMP. NONE OF US WANTED TO LEAVE BUT WE STAYED AS LONG AS WE COULD, OUR LIVES BACK HOME NEEDED ATTENTION. WE'D EXPERIENCED SOMETHING ENTIRELY UNIQUE AND THE ENERGY WAS *POWERFUL*.

I SAW THINGS, HEARD THINGS, FELT THINGS THAT I CANNOT PROPERLY CONVEY. *MAGIC* THINGS. THE THINGS I GREW UP BELIEVING BUT LOST SOMEWHERE - WAKING UP IN MY MIND AND MY HEART.

WITHIN A DAY I'D FORGOTTEN *FACEBOOK, TWITTER*, SOCIAL MEDIA IN GENERAL. I WORKED AND ATE AND LAUGHED WITH MY FELLOWS AND KNEW *PEACE*. IN A TIME OF GRIEF AND WOE I FOUND HOPE AND STRENGTH.

FOR A TIME, I WAS EXACTLY WHERE I BELONGED.

I CAME HOME BUT COULDN'T SHAKE THE CAMP. AT THANKSGIVING I WENT BACK ALONE, BUT IT HAD CHANGED.

THERE WERE MANY PEOPLE NOW, TOO MANY FOR THE MESSAGE TO STAY PURE. I WAS TURNED AWAY FROM THE TENTS I'D HELP SET UP AND SLEPT IN THE JEEP, FREEZING.

I FOUND LISA AND MY FRIENDS AND STAYED IN A TIPI WITH THEM THE NEXT NIGHT, IT WAS WARM IN THERE AND I WAS SOON ASLEEP. DEEP IN A FORGOTTEN DREAM, I WAS SHOCKED AWAKE BY A CRY IN THE CAMP. "*FIRE! FIRE!*"

RUBBING THE SLEEP FROM MY EYES I LOOKED UP AND SAW CORLEE RUN OUT WITH A FIRE EXTINGUISHER. A FEW MINUTES LATER SHE RETURNED. "IT'S ALL GOOD."

THE CAMP MIGHT HAVE CHANGED, BUT THEIR *WARRIORS'* HEARTS HAD NOT.

I WENT TO GIVE WHAT I COULD
AND INSTEAD, I TOOK .

I TOOK HOME A **FIRE** IN MY SPIRIT
  AN **AWAKENING** OF **HOPE** - POSSIBILITY

THE FIRE WILL **FADE** AND MY **HEART**
  WILL **FLOUNDER** - BUT I CANNOT **FORGET**

THERE IS **ALWAYS** A HIGHER ROAD
  THAN THE ONE I AM ON

IT IS THERE IF MY EYES AND HEART ARE OPEN

AND IF I HAVE THE **COURAGE** TO TAKE IT.

HOME. THE NATION NO LONGER FELT LIKE HOME, IT FELT INVADED. A BARRAGE OF EXECUTIVE ORDERS GREETED THE NEW YEAR, EACH MORE DREADFUL THAN THE LAST. THE *CATS* COMFORTED ME.

YES? WELL? SAY SOMETHING. IT'S JUST US—YOU CAN TALK, I KNOW IT...

IT WAS A TOUGH YEAR. A GLIMPSE OF THE NEWS WOULD RUIN MY DAY, AND THE PRESIDENT'S *FACE* WOULD HAUNT ME LONGER. I MARCHED IN *D.C.* FOR THE WATER PROTECTORS AND SAW *LISA, ELVIA,* AND *CORLEE* AGAIN BUT IT ALL FELT PRETTY USELESS.

WHILE THERE I STOPPED AT THE *NATIVE AMERICAN MUSEUM* AND SAW THE CHRONOLOGY OF BROKEN TREATIES. IT WAS ALL SHOCKINGLY DEPRESSING.

I PARTICIPATED IN *ACLU* FUNDRAISERS AND WHATEVER OTHER WAYS I COULD *RESIST* AND LOST FRIENDS OR CUT OFF *FAMILY* OVER CONFLICTING *BELIEFS* AND IDEOLOGIES.

HOW CAN YOU SUPPORT THIS EVIL SHIT??

I THOUGHT I *KNEW* YOU!

SOCIAL MEDIA SCROLLING FELL OFF—I'D SHARE *ART* AND THEN VANISH. MY CLOSE FRIENDS WERE ALL I FELT COMFORTABLE AROUND.

HOPELESS AND HELPLESS! I WAKE UP ANGRY EVERY DAY!

YOU AND ANYONE WITH HALF A BRAIN, LAD.

THERE'S GOTTA BE SOMETHING...

I STILL HIT THREE MEETINGS A WEEK AND WAS SPONSORING GUYS BUT THE SILVER LINING HAD BECOME A DULL CHEER, HARD TO BELIEVE IN.

YOU MIGHT FEEL LIKE *SHIT*... BUT JUST TRY AND REMEMBER-A DRINK WILL ONLY MAKE IT WORSE.

THE RELIEF IS NOT REAL. WE'VE GOTTA EARN IT NOW.

FUUUCK.

YEAH. I KNOW.

AMAZINGLY, I *DID* BELIEVE WHAT I WAS SAYING. AT SOME POINT "HIGHER POWER" BECAME "MY CREATOR" AND IT WAS *MY* JOB TO HONOR THE GIFT OF MY LIFE.

IT NO LONGER *MATTERED* IF "THE CREATOR" WAS REAL.

EACH DAY I THANKED IT AND I MADE SURE I MEANT IT EVERY GODDAMN TIME.

GO AWAY, CATS!

OKAY, YOU CAN STAY.

I FOUND *ESCAPE* AND *HEALING* IN MY WORK. I BEGAN AN EPIC *FANTASY* AND POURED MYSELF INTO IT.

THESE CHARACTERS ARE IN A HOPELESS SITUATION BUT THEY REFUSE TO GIVE UP! THEY'RE BETTER THAN ME.

MAYBE A HOPEFUL TALE WILL HELP.

A CONVENTION CALLED INDIGENOUS POP X CAUGHT MY EYE AND I WENT TO ALBEQUERQUE TO ATTEND. IT FED MY *SPIRIT* AND I'VE PARTICIPATED EVERY YEAR SINCE.

DAMN...THIS GUY IS *SUPER* NATIVE... WELL, LET'S GET THE TOUGH GUY THING OVER WITH ALREADY.

YOU DREW ALL THIS?

YUP.

... DAMN BRO, THIS IS GOOD STUFF.

?!? THAT'S RIGHT! WE'RE ALL NERDS HERE!

THANKS, MAN.

ELENA WAS MAKING A NAME FOR HERSELF AS AN INDIGENOUS *CHEF* AND ATTENDED ONE YEAR. WE DROVE OUT TO SEE THE *CLIFF DWELLINGS.*

WOW.

YUP.

ANGER, HOWEVER, WAS EATING ME UP INSIDE. I WAS TORN ABOUT SOME PERSONAL MATTERS THAT FELT OUT OF MY CONTROL AND ENDED UP IN THE DELLS, ATTENDING A SACRED *CEREMONY.*

MY ANGER IS KEEPING ME FROM APPRECIATING BEING HERE.

HELL, I DON'T KNOW WHAT'S GOING ON HERE ANYWAY. WHY AM I EVEN *HERE?*

I WANDERED FROM THE *PRAYER LODGE* AND INTO THE MOONLIGHT... I DIDN'T UNDERSTAND HALF OF WHAT WAS GOING ON AND FELT *APART* FROM IT.

THE SMELL OF *WOODSMOKE* WAS STRONG AND I COULD HEAR *DRUMS* AND *SINGING.* THE TREES WERE BLACK AND IT COULD HAVE BEEN A THOUSAND YEARS AGO AS I DROPPED TO MY KNEES, OVERWHELMED.

CREATOR—I DON'T EXPECT ANSWERS. I CAN MAKE UP MY OWN MIND.

BUT PLEASE,...LIFT THIS ANGER FROM MY HEART, SO I MIGHT SEE THINGS *CLEARLY.*

A DELICATE RING OF *LIGHT* HOVERED AROUND MY SHADOW'S HEAD, AND STAYED THERE— NO MATTER HOW I MOVED... IT STAYED.

I ROSE, EMBARRASSED AND WORRIED SOMEONE MIGHT HAVE SEEN ME. THEN I GLIMPSED MY *MOON SHADOW* IN THE GRASS.

WEIRD.

I TOLD EVENA ABOUT IT THE NEXT DAY.

YEAH, I LOOKED IT UP. I GUESS IT'S A KIND OF *RARE* PHENOMENON. KINDA RARE.

GUESS THE FULL MOON... SOMETHING ABOUT THE DEW OR MOISTURE LEVEL...

A TRICK OF THE LIGHT THAT OCCURS WHEN ALL THE CONDITIONS CONVERGE IN JUST THE—*WHY ARE YOU LAUGHING?*

HMMM.

YEAH, IT MIGHT BE ALL THOSE THINGS. BUT ISN'T IT SOMETHING, ALL THOSE ELEMENTS COMING TOGETHER WHEN YOU *NEEDED A SIGN?* CAN'T *SCIENCE* BE ANOTHER TOOL TO LET YOU KNOW YOUR PRAYER WAS *ACKNOWLEDGED?*

HUH.

TO ME THAT WAS A COSMIC, MIND-BLOWING REVELATION.
THOSE INSANE, LONELY DRUNKEN NIGHTS WEREN'T FAR OFF.
EVERYTHING DID LEAD TO THIS MOMENT, THIS VERY MOMENT.
AS I WRITE THIS, AS YOU READ THIS.
          EVERYTHING.
EVERY CHANCE TAKEN, EVERY MUSICAL NOTE,
ALL THE FRIENDS MADE AND LOST
EVERY LOVE, THE CHANCE ENCOUNTERS ON BRIDGES
IN BARS IN CLASS AT WORK OR NOT MEANING TO
RECOVERY AFTER DESPAIR, EVERY MOMENT OF DREAD
          WATCHING A LOVED ONE BREATHE IN SLEEP
THE KINDNESSES, A KISS, A HUG, HOLDING A HAND
STOLEN GLANCES MISSED OPPORTUNITIES REGRETS
SICKNESS AND DEATH AND EVERY FILM WATCHED
EVERY BOOK READ EVERY PAGE DRAWN EVERY MEAL
ALL THE FIGHTS LOST AND HATE ENDURED
          SWEATING OUT A SICKNESS
CRAZY HORSE IN DEFIANCE RED CLOUD IN PRAYER
MY FATHER PLAYING THE BASS HIS BROTHERS DYING
CHIEF BIG FOOT CROSSING THE BADLANDS MY MOTHER
MY MOTHER CALLING ME TO TELL ME HOW OLD TONY'D BE
CHIEF BIG FOOT MURDERED AND FROZEN IN THE SNOW
          STEALING GRANPA'S GLASSES
MY SISTER BECOMING A LEADER, EVERY SUNRISE
MY OTHER SISTER A MOTHER, EVERY RAINDROP
TRAGEDY HISTORY LIES TRIUMPHS LOSS
LOST CAUSES ALL REBELLION ALL OF IT
EVERY MOMENT IN TIME, TIME ITSELF
          BEYOND MAN, BEYOND TIME
MIRACLES. TRAGEDIES. ALL LEADING
TO THIS MOMENT. YOU READING OPENING
YOUR MIND TO MINE. HEARING MY THOUGHTS,
HEARING MY STORY. SEEING MY WEAKNESS
          MY STRENGTH
LET US OPEN OUR HEARTS AND
BE CONNECTED.

EVERYTHING HAS LED
UP TO NOW.

WHAT DO WE DO
WITH IT?

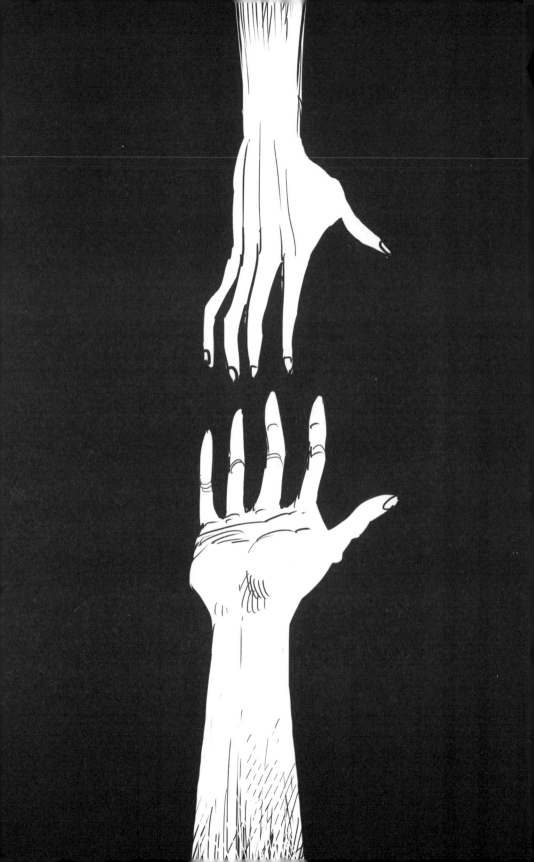

COME HOME,
INDIO

AUTHOR'S NOTE

In the creation of this book, there were a few issues I struggled with. And I'd like to take a second to share some of my thoughts on them.

As I was writing this memoir I realized some serious omissions had to be made. Significant moments and people close to me were left out, either for the sake of brevity, or because I thought those people wouldn't want to be represented in a book. Some folks told me they wanted to remain private, and I did my best to respect that. But I'd like to acknowledge that many good people were kept out of the mix, and this in no way indicates that they weren't important to me.

Another thing I want to address is the language used in the book. I realize quite a bit of it is harsh and might be triggering. In discussions with my editor, I considered changing things so as to make it less offensive. But in the end, I felt it was necessary to leave that ugliness in there, because racism and homophobia were slung about so casually by people in my life when I was growing up, that pretending this wasn't the case seems a disservice to all those who, like me, suffered from those barbs.

Finally, I take great care in my daily life, and certainly in anything I create, not to advertise or represent the specific program by which I got sober. To paraphrase a great author of horror books, however, I will say, "If you look in a phone book it'll probably be at the very front of the alphabet."

Please take care,

Jim Terry
Chicago, Illinois
June 2020